T0403235

EVERYDAY PRAYERS

— FOR —

CHRISTMAS

The Light that Was and Is and Is to Come

STACEY THACKER

WHITAKER
HOUSE

EVERYDAY PRAYERS FOR CHRISTMAS
The Light that Was and Is and Is to Come

staceythacker.com
www.instagram.com/staceythacker
x.com/staceythacker

ISBN: 979-8-88769-439-9
eBook ISBN: 979-8-88769-440-5
Printed in Colombia
© 2025 by Stacey Thacker

Whitaker House
1030 Hunt Valley Circle
New Kensington, PA 15068
www.whitakerhouse.com

Library of Congress Cataloging-in-Publication Data
Names: Thacker, Stacey, 1971- author
Title: Everyday prayers for Christmas : the light that was and is and is to
   come / Stacey Thacker.
Description: New Kensington, PA : Whitaker House, [2025] | Summary: "A
   devotional and reflective journal written especially for women that uses
   Scripture readings to pray to God, designed to help readers experience
   the light of Jesus and share the joy of His birth with others especially
   during the Christmas season"— Provided by publisher.
Identifiers: LCCN 2025008539 (print) | LCCN 2025008540 (ebook) | ISBN
   9798887694399 trade paperback | ISBN 9798887694405 ebook
Subjects: LCSH: Christmas—Prayers and devotions | Christian women—Prayers
   and devotions | LCGFT: Prayers
Classification: LCC BV45 .T447 2025 (print) | LCC BV45 (ebook) | DDC
   242/.335—dc23/eng/20250524
LC record available at https://lccn.loc.gov/2025008539
LC ebook record available at https://lccn.loc.gov/2025008540

1 2 3 4 5 6 7 8 9 10 11 ⨆ 32 31 30 29 28 27 26 25

But as for me, I will look to the LORD;
I will wait for the God of my salvation;
my God will hear me.

Rejoice not over me, O my enemy;
when I fall, I shall rise;
when I sit in darkness,
the LORD will be a light to me.

—Micah 7:7–8

CONTENTS

FOREWORD

Last year, it became clear to us that we needed a new Christmas tree. Our youngest son is allergic to real trees, so we have an artificial tree. The one we'd had for over a decade was in sad shape from years of abuse by our rescue kitty, Nermal, who was named after one of the neighborhood cats in the Garfield cartoons.

Nermal adores the Christmas tree. When the tree comes out, something comes over our beautiful, pure white cat, who has a bit of an attitude problem throughout the rest of the year. It becomes *his* tree. He climbs up and makes it his winter home. When we add our collection of Hallmark singing snowmen under the tree, they become *his* people. He sleeps among them, peering out at us from his village of almost look-alike comrades. Up and down he goes, from the snowmen to his favorite branches, and his antics, while delightful to watch, have completely worn out our tree.

He was severely malnourished when my husband, Cory, found him in a mud puddle on the side of the road. Not anymore. The spots in the Christmas tree where Nermal likes to nestle for hours have started to sag badly under his growing weight. While the lights and ornaments hid the sad state of the branches beautifully at night, it looked horrible during the day. No strategic placement on my part could cure the fact that the artificial branches had buckled and bent under our pretty kitty.

That Christmas, when my father-in-law was visiting us for dinner one evening, he noticed the sad state of our family tree and offered to give us one of my mother-in-law's trees. This was no small offer. My mother-in-law, Linda, loved Christmas. She had three separate Christmas trees, one for each of her sons and their families, and took great pleasure in getting each of us entirely too many gifts. Christmas was undeniably her favorite time of the year. Under those trees were piles of packages all wrapped in matching paper with beautiful ribbons and bows—a visual feast that caused her six grandchildren's eyes to dance with glee and anticipation. Those trees, with their visible display of love stacked underneath, lit up her home.

Linda has been in assisted living for a few years now. In her late sixties, dementia and Parkinson's disease began to take her from us. Her decline, especially at such a young age, has been hard for those who love her most, especially at Christmas. We miss her traditions and excitement over the spirit of the season, and even though she's still with us bodily, we miss all that made her, *her*. To have one of her trees—a beautiful, full, pre-lit tree we probably would never have splurged on ourselves—would be a treasure.

Normally, I'm against any Christmas before Thanksgiving. But my husband would start listening to Christmas music in September if he could, so we usually compromise, agreeing that he can listen to it all he wants in his car, but not in mine and not in the house. Not before Thanksgiving. But that year, it felt like our hearts could use a little a bit more light. So we put the tree up in early November and enjoyed the soft, beautiful reminder of my mother-in-law's deep love for Christmas and her family all season long.

One night, as I sat just staring at the tree in an otherwise dark room, a habit of mine during the holidays, I had a thought. We talk about Jesus more openly and freely at Christmas than any other time of the year. It's the time when most of the world, in some form or fashion, celebrates that Jesus came.

But do they know Jesus came *for them?*

Jesus said, *"I am the light of the world. Whoever follows me will not walk in darkness, but will have the light of life"* (John 8:12).

That's the heart of the book you now hold in your hands. When Stacey Thacker came to me with the idea of making it a journey through Jesus's role as the Light, I knew it would be a blessing, not only because there's so much biblical significance to the concept, but also because Stacey has lived it. She's seen darkness and chosen to live in the light only Jesus can give. I admire a lot of things about her, but that tops the list. She just chooses Jesus over and over again, despite the opportunities to dwell in darkness.

Jesus came for you, for me, and for anyone who allows the light of life He freely offers to invade the darkness of sin and death. It's deeply personal. We were lost without Him, and now we are found, but this isn't just about salvation. It's about every moment of every day, and Christmas is the time to reflect on and celebrate that with abandon, not just in the gifts we give, but in the thoughts we think, the offerings we give, and the way we live.

May you live in the Light.

—*Brooke McGlothlin*

Founder, Million Praying Moms
Author, *Everyday Prayers for Peace*

INTRODUCTION

Do you ever feel like you don't know what to pray at Christmastime? As the calendar turns from November to December, do you think, "How am I going to celebrate this important season with my family when I am already weary?"

God wants something more for us than temporary holiday fixes and feel-good moments. He wants us to walk with Him in the light and bring others with us.

From Genesis through Revelation, God has used light to pierce the darkness, to cause things to grow, and to show us the way. The apostle John connects Jesus as both the *light* and the Word. He is the Word made flesh who came to dwell among us. He is the light of the world who overcame darkness through His life, death, and resurrection. As believers, we have a personal relationship with Him who came in power and gives us true *hope* and *light*. Lately, I've felt overwhelmed by the darkness in our world. But I am reminded today, as we look toward Christmas, that where God dwells, there is light.

And light has always been a symbol of hope.

I love that Jesus talked about light too. The Message Bible puts it this way: "*I am the world's Light. No one who follows me stumbles around in the darkness. I provide plenty of light to live in*" (John 8:12 MSG). Jesus came to show us the way. Maybe celebrating Christmas feels hard this year and as lights are being hung on the tree, you can't help but think about your busy schedule, the gifts that you need to purchase, and the treats that you want to bake. Distractions pull at you from every side. Maybe you are unsure of how to celebrate the birth of Christ in a meaningful way with your family. I get it—I truly do. Christmas sometimes feels more like a bigger to-do list than a season of anticipation. I'd like to offer you something a little bit different this year. I want to invite you to join me for a thirty-one-day prayer journey.

Together, we are going behold the light that was, is, and is to come.

Jesus being the light of the world means that where He dwells, there is light and hope. When we are weary, we need to be able to *see* from the perspective of God, who knows all and sees all. We need to remember that in Christ, we have plenty of light to live in. And the world can't overcome it. Not at Christmas, nor on any other day for that matter. This Christmas, let's quietly move in the direction of the light and pray for the life He came to give us to shine brightly for all the world to see.

Let the light in, my friend.

Stacey Thacker

Note: This devotional uses Million Praying Moms' "Think, Pray, Praise" method of daily prayer. If you are not familiar with this prayer practice, please visit: www.millionprayingmoms.com/the-think-pray-praise-method-of-daily-prayer

DAY 1

THE BOUNDARY
LINES ARE DRAWN

In the beginning, God created the heavens and the earth.
The earth was without form and void, and darkness was over
the face of the deep. And the Spirit of God was hovering over
the face of the waters. And God said, "Let there be light," and
there was light. And God saw that the light was good. And God
separated the light from the darkness.
— Genesis 1:1–4

It seems to be hardwired into our DNA that light is good, and darkness is not. We don't have to be taught to be afraid of the dark. Even as babies, all of my girls needed night-lights at bedtime. During the Christmas season, we substituted those singular white lights for tiny Christmas trees. And to be honest, we were sad to take them down in January.

Light has a way of calming our anxious hearts no matter how old we are. When my husband traveled for work years ago and was out of town, it was common for me to promise my girls that they were perfectly safe at night … and then go to bed with my bathroom light on. The light streaming out under the closed bathroom door gave me a sense of security.

The darkness holds obscurity and omens.

But light brings comfort and courage.

And so, from a young age, we push back the darkness with whatever light we can find, we call it good, and we rest in it.

SOMETHING TO THINK ABOUT

In Genesis, the book of beginnings, we learn that God formed the universe and everything in it, bringing order, form, and function to the chaos and confusion of the cosmos. He filled the world with His goodness. I love how theologian Judith Odor states this:

> At the heart of Old Testament's symbolic use of light and darkness is the connection the text makes between light and the personal presence of God, and darkness as all that opposes God. This link begins as early as Gen 1:2, where God creates light to serve as a boundary to darkness.[1]

The first good thing that God created was light and immediately this good thing was separated from the darkness. It was a distinctive boundary line drawn physically between:

+ Light and darkness
+ Clarity and chaos
+ Filled and empty

God spoke light into the inky blackness first so that we would never doubt that where He dwelled, there was light.

And the light was good.

EXTRA VERSES FOR STUDY OR PRAYER

Psalm 139:11–12; Romans 1:20

VERSE OF THE DAY

And God said, "Let there be light," and there was light.
                                                    —Genesis 1:3

---

1. Judith A. Odor, "Light and Darkness," ed. John D. Barry et al., *The Lexham Bible Dictionary* (Bellingham, WA: Lexham Press, 2016).

PRAYER

Father, thank You that You brought order to the void from the very beginning of the universe. You began with light to remind us that You are always with us. This Christmas, we don't have to be afraid of the darkness because the light of Your presence pierces it completely. May we rest in Your goodness today. In Jesus's name, amen.

THINK

PRAY

PRAISE

TO-DO

PRAYER LIST

QUESTIONS FOR DEEPER REFLECTION

1. Have you ever lost power for more than a few hours and had to depend on other forms of light such as candles or flashlights? What did you notice?

2. How did God create light on day one? Why do you think this is significant?

DAY 2

A MIRACULOUS LIGHT IN THE WILDERNESS

And the LORD went before them by day in a pillar of cloud to lead them along the way, and by night in a pillar of fire to give them light, that they might travel by day and by night.
—Exodus 13:21

About eight years into our marriage, my husband was offered a job in Central Florida. That may sound magical, but for me it meant moving over a thousand miles away to a place where I didn't know a single person. To top it off, I had a three-year-old and was eight weeks away from delivering my second daughter, who was due just after Christmas. I didn't want to go. It felt like entering a wilderness.

As I unpacked boxes in my new home that November and looked at the calendar, I knew we were drawing closer not only to welcoming our new baby but also celebrating Christmas. I wanted a new tradition to mark our journey as a family. I wanted to be able to look back and say, "This is for us, for our little family. We are here in the place God has led us, and He has been faithful."

About that time, I read an article in a magazine about Advent and lighting candles of anticipation to direct our hearts toward the coming of Jesus. It seemed easy enough to implement with my growing girth and my bubbly toddler. And so, I picked up some greenery, four red taper candles, and one larger white candle to make our first Advent display. Each Sunday night between Thanksgiving and

Christmas, we would light a candle, tell the story of Christmas, and give small gifts to each other.

We've been celebrating Advent as a family ever since. Our original party of three grew in a few weeks to four with the birth of our second daughter. Over the next seven years, we added two more girls, which multiplied our joy. But I will always remember that first Christmas in Florida over twenty-two years ago, when my heart ached for home, the wilderness felt blinding, and I looked for the light of Christmas to point me toward the One who went before me every step of the way.

SOMETHING TO THINK ABOUT

When God's people were rescued from hundreds of years of captivity out of Egypt, He didn't lead them to the land of promise by the shortest and most obvious route. Instead, God led them by way of the wilderness toward a sea that they could not cross without His mighty hand of deliverance. God had a reason for taking them the long way. The land in between Egypt and Canaan, their new home, was filled with enemies. He did this to protect them from a war they were not prepared to fight.

During the day, God led His people with a towering cloud that extended high above them. When the cloud miraculously moved, God's people did too. This protective covering worked well in the wilderness by day. But at night, the darkness of the desert would be oppressive. How would the people see God's presence? How would they know the way? God answered this by replacing the cloud with a pillar of fire every night to split open the darkness and declare to everyone who could see that He was both guiding and guarding His people. Scripture goes on to tell us, *"The pillar of cloud by day and the pillar of fire by night did not depart from before the people"* (Exodus 13:22).

Maybe you feel like you are in a wilderness place today. Perhaps you are lonely and your heart is aching for home or the way things used to be. I want you to know that you can ask God for a miraculous light in the wilderness too. He is the same yesterday, today, and forever. (See Hebrews 13:8.) He leads us still. It might not be seen visibly out the window of your minivan as you drive around town, but the light still shines, pointing the way to the birth of the Christ child, who came to show us the way to the Father.

And the light will not depart from us.

EXTRA VERSES FOR STUDY OR PRAYER
Hebrews 13:5

VERSE OF THE DAY

And the Lord went before them by day in a pillar of cloud to lead them along the way, and by night in a pillar of fire to give them light, that they might travel by day and by night.
—Exodus 13:21

PRAYER

Father, You always go before me, and I am grateful for the intentional way You lead me, especially when I feel alone. I realize that the path might not be the easy way, but Your abiding presence will always be with me. In Jesus's name, amen.

THINK

PRAY

PRAISE

_____

_____

_____

TO-DO

_____

_____

_____

PRAYER LIST

_____

_____

_____

QUESTIONS FOR DEEPER REFLECTION

1. What Christmas traditions have you celebrated over the years that help point you toward the true meaning of the season? What do you love most about them and why?

_____

_____

_____

2. How does God's abiding presence bring you comfort today?

_____

_____

_____

DAY 3

EXPERIENCING THE STORY OF LIGHT

The LORD spoke to Moses, saying, "Command the people of Israel to bring you pure oil from beaten olives for the lamp, that a light may be kept burning regularly. Outside the veil of the testimony, in the tent of meeting, Aaron shall arrange it from evening to morning before the LORD regularly. It shall be a statute forever throughout your generations. He shall arrange the lamps on the lampstand of pure gold before the LORD regularly."
—Leviticus 24:1–4

"Honey, isn't anyone going to come and visit you and your baby?" the nurse asked me as she finished swaddling my newborn and handed her to me. "No." I choked out through tears. "We just recently moved here, and I don't know anyone." She patted my arm and promised to visit me every day. And she did.

Our second baby girl arrived five days before Christmas. She was healthy and whole. Honestly, I didn't have anything to complain about. But as we left the hospital, I was trying to figure out how we were going to celebrate Christmas with a newborn. To top it off, I had done zero Christmas shopping for our family. I was hurting—physically and emotionally—and felt hidden. I thought maybe God had forgotten about me. I whispered a simple prayer, and we loaded up our van and drove home.

When we arrived at our neighborhood, I couldn't believe what I saw. Lining the streets were a thousand tiny candles in white paper bags leading all the way to our driveway. It was beautiful. I found out later that this was an annual Christmas tradition in our community. But what are the chances that this would be perfectly timed for our arrival home with our new baby? There was light pointing us toward hope and home from our gentle, loving Shepherd, who whispered to me, "I see you. And everything is going to be okay."

SOMETHING TO THINK ABOUT

When the Lord spoke to Moses regarding the oil for the lampstand that would illuminate the tabernacle, He commanded that the people bring the purest kind of olive oil. These drops of liquid gold were not extracted from a large press using heat. They were taken from broken and bruised pieces of ripe olives and pressed by hand into a small mortar with a pestle. Drop by drop, the oil was collected by individuals who would contribute to the ongoing inner work of the tabernacle, ensuring that God's servants would never be in darkness but be bathed in precious light.

Maybe God invited His people to engage in this laborious work of oil collection and offering so that they would be able to experience the story of light themselves. Instead of merely gazing at a miraculous light, their hands would drip with the oil that would light the way to the very presence of God.

The hope-filled light would burn always.

EXTRA VERSES FOR STUDY OR PRAYER

Exodus 27:20–21; 2 Corinthians 4:8–10

VERSE OF THE DAY

Command the people of Israel to bring you pure oil from beaten olives for the lamp, that a light may be kept burning regularly.
—Leviticus 24:2

PRAYER

Father, remind us that even when we are hurting and hard-pressed, the most precious testimony can come from our lives. May we focus on Your Word and through prayer fan the flame of Your Spirit so others can see hope burning brightly. In Jesus's name, amen.

THINK

PRAY

PRAISE

TO-DO

PRAYER LIST

QUESTIONS FOR DEEPER REFLECTION

1. If your circumstances are making the celebration of Christmas hard this year, how can you shift your perspective and invite God to point you toward His presence?

2. What do you do to experience light daily?

3. Why do you think God asked His people for the purest olive oil? What did this represent?

DAY 4

LOOK UPON
THE LIGHT

He has redeemed my soul from going down into the pit,
and my life shall look upon the light.
—Job 33:28

You probably don't naturally gravitate to the book of Job during the Christmas season as you sit by the tree, drink hot cocoa, and listen to carols. Considered by many biblical scholars to be the oldest written book of the Bible, Job tells the tragic story of a man who lost everything rather suddenly through no fault of his own, the mostly inadequate counsel of his friends, and how he met God during his deepest, darkest pain. Ironically, it is also a book soaked in light. Job has more than thirty references to light in forty-two chapters. I find this fascinating. How can a book about suffering also point us toward the light?

SOMETHING TO THINK ABOUT

In our verse of the day, Elihu is speaking to Job. And though not everything he says is perfect, he does make a case for why God allows suffering. In the end, he reminds Job that God is a rescuer and redeemer who allows suffering in our lives to refine us and make us like Him, using suffering for our good, not to punish us. In doing so, Elihu lifts Job's gaze to the light, reminding him to simply look up to God.

God also has a speech for Job that helps him to see life from a different perspective. Job has asked many questions, so God has some questions for him as well:

Have you ever commanded the morning to appear and caused the dawn to rise in the east? Have you made daylight spread to the ends of the earth, to bring an end to the night's wickedness? As the light approaches, the earth takes shape like clay pressed beneath a seal; it is robed in brilliant colors. The light disturbs the wicked and stops the arm that is raised in violence. … Where does light come from, and where does darkness go? Can you take each to its home? Do you know how to get there?
—Job 38:12–15, 19–20 NLT

Job ultimately takes comfort in the God who commands the morning to appear and spreads daylight to the ends of the earth. Only God knows where the light comes from and where the darkness goes when the light enters in. Job knows he cannot do these things, but the One who does control the light can absolutely be trusted. We can also take comfort in knowing that every question Job asked in darkness was answered when Jesus was born. He is the fulfillment of every analogy to light in Scripture. Everything changes in our lives when we fix our gaze on Him.

Because the light changes our perspective.

EXTRA VERSES FOR STUDY OR PRAYER
Genesis 1:5; Genesis 1:18

VERSE OF THE DAY

He has redeemed my soul from going down into the pit, and my life shall look upon the light. —Job 33:28

PRAYER

Father, sometimes we can best see the light in the shadowed times of darkness. Remind me during this season of light to be a testimony to others who are struggling. May I be a good friend who encourages the downtrodden to look up. And if that person is me, continue to remind me each morning where the *light* comes from. In Jesus's name, amen.

THINK

PRAY

PRAISE

TO-DO   PRAYER LIST

QUESTIONS FOR DEEPER REFLECTION

1. When was the last time you saw a sunrise and were filled with awe?

2. What is one simple way you can remind yourself to look upon the light this Christmas?

DAY 5

WHERE FEAR MEETS ITS MATCH

The LORD is my light and my salvation; whom shall I fear? The LORD is the stronghold of my life; of whom shall I be afraid?
—Psalm 27:1

I recently read an interesting fact about the human eye. Supposedly, under the right nighttime conditions, the human eye can see the light of a single candle up to fourteen miles away. Apparently, it depends on the landscape, atmospheric conditions, and the brightness of the candle for the flame to be seen at this distance. Even so, our fearfully and wonderfully made eyes seem to be programmed to search for light, whether it's fourteen miles away or beside our bed on the darkest night. This should be easier at Christmastime more than any time of year because light suddenly appears everywhere our eyes can see.

I don't know how your town celebrates, but I'm always amazed at how my drive home after a long day at work just feels different in December. Do you want a street to give others feelings of joy and peace? Just string lights in the trees and hang massive ornaments all around your town square. That's what our hometown does—and every chance we get, we start at one end of the street and drive slowly to the other side, smiling and singing all the way.

SOMETHING TO THINK ABOUT

In Hebrew literature, light is often seen as a metaphor for deliverance. In Psalm 27, David proclaims that the answer to his fear is light. But this is no ordinary light. The light that overcomes his fear is the *Lord*. He is both a Savior and a shelter in his distress. David knew that God's presence in times of trouble soothes us because He is a safe, light-filled place we can hide. For David, it didn't matter if his enemy was an army surrounding him or a lion in the wilderness. The answer is clear when David asks, *"Whom shall I fear?"* He can't and won't name an enemy; sheltered in the light of his Savior, David's faith is firm, and he is not afraid.

I wonder if we have such confidence in the Lord when our hearts are anxious and unsettled. Is He the one thing we seek? Do our spiritual eyes look for His light in the darkness, hungry for His presence? David promises us at the end of this psalm that we can and should wait expectantly for the Lord. He will come, bringing His glorious light with Him, and fear will once and for all meet its match.

Oh, that we would have faith eyes to see it.

EXTRA VERSES FOR STUDY OR PRAYER

Psalm 27:14; Philippians 4:8

VERSE OF THE DAY

The Lord is my light and my salvation; whom shall I fear? The Lord is the stronghold of my life; of whom shall I be afraid?
—Psalm 27:1

PRAYER

Father, send Your light today. I confess that I am fearful of what the day may bring. I am easily distracted by the cares of this world. Thank You that You made my eyes to look for light. Here, now, in this chaotic world, may my spiritual eyes look for Your salvation that I may have a firm and fearless faith. In Jesus's name, amen.

THINK

PRAY

PRAISE

TO-DO

PRAYER LIST

QUESTIONS FOR DEEPER REFLECTION

1. What do your eyes naturally search for when you are fearful?

2. How have you waited for the Lord and His light to come recently?

_____

_____

_____

3. Who do you need to encourage to look for the light?

_____

_____

_____

LIGHT LIKE A GARMENT

Bless the LORD, O my soul! O LORD my God,
you are very great! You are clothed with splendor and majesty,
covering yourself with light as with a garment,
stretching out the heavens like a tent.
—Psalm 104:1–2

Several years ago, I had an opportunity to have a special dress made for a Christmas program at my church. Our Singing Christmas Trees were well known all over Central Florida and attracted tens of thousands of people. One year, I auditioned for a vocal part in a trio and much to my surprise got the call to sing the part. This trio included two gentlemen who were both named Steve. They were asked to wear tuxedos for the seven live performances, while I was asked to obtain a formal dress.

One of Steves was an exceptionally talented tailor. After a rehearsal, he asked me if I had found a dress. When I said, "Not yet," he generously offered to make a dress for me using some extra fabric he had at home. I couldn't say yes quick enough! A week or so later, without taking one measurement, Steve produced the dress: a stunning two-piece ensemble made from brown velvet with coordinating taffeta. The skirt had a gorgeous extension that trailed behind me when I walked. I was so moved by his talent, I teared up in the dressing room as I tried it on. It fit almost perfectly and only needed a couple of small adjustments.

I've never forgotten how it made me feel to wear this beautiful dress throughout the run of the show. Certainly, this was not an everyday occurrence for me as a stay-at-home mom of three little ones. I knew it would likely never happen again, so I soaked up every minute.

SOMETHING TO THINK ABOUT

The writer of Psalm 104 needs only a few sentences to reorient our souls to the grandeur and majesty of our Creator. With an echo back to Genesis 1, he shifts our attention to the idea that God effortlessly wraps Himself in the first element of creation—light—and He wears it like a garment. This soul-stirring picture reminds us that light is evidence of His divine glory. Though distinct from His creation, God is intimately involved with and takes great delight in every aspect of it. Remember, He called everything He made good. And so it is.

Charles Spurgeon once said:

The conception is sublime: but it makes us feel how altogether inconceivable the personal glory of the Lord must be; if light itself is but his garment and veil, what must be the blazing splendour of his own essential being! We are lost in astonishment and dare not pry into the mystery lest we be blinded by its insufferable glory.[2]

When was the last time you paused to simply adore the greatness of our God? I know the season is busy. I know you have extra items on your to-do list. But this psalm can serve as a holy pause to point you to the One who has heaven as His home, earth as His footstool, and a garment of light that would dazzle even a Disney princess. *"Bless the* Lord, *O my soul!"*

He is worthy of every song I could possibly sing. And more.

2. C. H. Spurgeon, *The Treasury of David, Vol. V* (London: Passmore and Alabaster, 1908), 2.

EXTRA VERSES FOR STUDY OR PRAYER
Genesis 1:3–4; Isaiah 66:1

VERSE OF THE DAY

You are clothed with splendor and majesty, covering yourself with light as with a garment, stretching out the heavens like a tent. —Psalm 104:1–2

PRAYER

Father, today we pause to remember that to You, light is but a garment You wear. This is a brilliant display of Your glory and a mystery our minds can't quite sort out. We simultaneously bow our knees and declare how great You truly are. In Jesus's name, amen.

THINK

PRAY

PRAISE

TO-DO

PRAYER LIST

QUESTIONS FOR DEEPER REFLECTION

1. Have you ever worn an exceptionally great dress? Maybe you made your flower girl debut at age five and felt like a princess. Perhaps your junior prom dress was a thing of beauty, or maybe your wedding dress was exactly what you always dreamed it would be. What was glorious about that dress and how did it make you feel?

2. Write a few sentences of praise describing God being clothed in a garment of light. How does this truth bring hope to you today?

DAY 7

A DAILY LIGHT

Your word is a lamp to my feet and
a light to my path.
—Psalm 119:105

One morning close to Christmas, I settled in my chair with my warmish cup of coffee and a collection of Advent readings. As I closed my eyes, I greeted the familiar ache that has been there for quite some time. Maybe even years. Sometimes life just hurts. Especially at Christmastime.

So what do we do when life hurts? Well first, we need to be honest with Jesus. He knows anyway. But we need to tell Him, and in the process, we pour out that ache bit by bit. The Bible has a name for this type of honesty. It's called lamenting. When we lament, we pour out our hearts to the Lord and tell Him exactly what we are feeling. But we don't stay stuck in that emotional purging. We need to shift our focus, start afresh, and behold Him through His Word. Because when we behold Jesus, it changes everything. And His Word is the perfect place to go to next.

SOMETHING TO THINK ABOUT

In ancient Hebrew cultures, a small house lamp was quite useful. Easily carried around and moved from place to place, this oil-burning lamp provided just enough light to see the tasks at hand for every member of the family. I love the imagery from our key verse today of the Word of God being carried *with us* throughout the day so we can see what we are doing and have just enough light to know the way to go. Elisabeth Elliot remembered this from her father:

> "A Christian who is saturated with the Word," my father wrote, "is likely to have a calm, wholesome outlook on life; to be kept steady in the path of God's will in either joy or sorrow, wealth or poverty; he is likely to be a pleasant companion, not voluble in aimless talk; and he will not be overly disturbed by world conditions."[3]

Does that sound like light to you? *Saturated. Calm. Wholesome. Steady. Pleasant.* God's Word provides all that and more. Maybe life has brought darkness or sorrow to you this Christmas. Perhaps your heart feels a bit aimless or even disturbed by what is happening in the chaotic world around you. May I encourage you with this gentle thought? Pick up the lamp of God's Word. Carry the light of His truth with you throughout the day. Let it saturate your very soul. Know that every reference to the Word points us to Jesus, who is the Author. And in the process, let His glorious light put you back together and show you the way to walk steadily forward.

EXTRA VERSES FOR STUDY OR PRAYER

Psalm 119:37; Hebrews 12:2

VERSE OF THE DAY

Your word is a lamp to my feet and a light to my path.
—Psalm 119:105

PRAYER

Father, thank You for Your Word, which points me to Jesus. May I fix my eyes on Him as the Author and Finisher of my faith. Let me carry Your light of truth with me today as I live, work, play, and celebrate His coming at Christmas. Show

---

3. Elisabeth Elliot, *The Shaping of a Christian Family: How My Parents Nurtured My Faith* (Ada, MI: Revell, 2023), 56.

me how to live for You and shine Your light to the world. In Jesus's name, amen.

THINK

PRAY

PRAISE

TO-DO

PRAYER LIST

QUESTIONS FOR DEEPER REFLECTION

1. Do you have a regular time in the Word? How is it different during the Christmas season?

------

2. What verse from the Bible steadies you and brings a sense of calm to your life? Write it here.

_____

_____

_____

3. Today, read from your physical Bible. Carry it with you from room to room as you go throughout your day as a reminder that God's Word is a light for our daily lives.

_____

_____

_____

DAY 8

THE LIGHT OF HOPE

*The people who walked in darkness
have seen a great light; those who dwelt in
a land of deep darkness,
on them has light shone.*
—Isaiah 9:2

Have you ever been in a place so dark you couldn't see your hand right in front of your face? Maybe you had to navigate your way in the dark through a minefield of toys to get to a crying child. In 2004, during a particularly turbulent hurricane season, my family was without power for several days straight. The darkness almost did me in. If our friends hadn't called on day five to say, "Hey, our power is back on, come on over," I might not be here today. I'm kidding. Mostly. But what I do know is that physical darkness, no matter how oppressive, is nothing compared to real spiritual darkness.

SOMETHING TO THINK ABOUT

Isaiah was a prophet sent to God's people to warn them to repent of their sins and prepare for His coming judgment. Yet sprinkled throughout the diverse collection of messages from God in the book of Isaiah, the prophet bursts forth with hope as well. Alongside his warning, he was also telling them that God had a plan to rescue and redeem them. He wasn't going to walk away. Instead, God would walk ahead of them, with them, and behind them in the darkness. And then, a great light would come. But for now, they had to wait.

If you look at our key verse today, you might notice a couple of things about the people Isaiah was speaking to:

+ They *walked* in darkness.
+ They *dwelt* in a land of deep darkness.

This wasn't a darkness they could escape. It pressed in on all sides. They lived and *pitched their tents* in a land of darkness that wanted to destroy them. At times, I wonder if it felt like their souls were being crushed. However, they were simultaneously learning that God was worthy of their trust even in the darkness. He was using these circumstances to draw His people toward Him in an extraordinary way. Just like physical light broke into the chaos and darkness at creation, the true light of the world would burst forth into the spiritual darkness, split it wide open, and shine upon them. Creation served to remind them that God says what He means and does what He says. And here was where their hope could rest.

God's people were promised light. They were looking for light. And in the waiting, their hope didn't diminish. It grew.

EXTRA VERSES FOR STUDY OR PRAYER
Isaiah 9:1; Matthew 4:13–16

VERSE OF THE DAY

The people who walked in darkness have seen a great light; those who dwelt in a land of deep darkness, on them has light shone.
—Isaiah 9:2

PRAYER

Father, thank You that waiting with hope doesn't diminish us but grows our capacity to experience Jesus and the joy He brings. Even when we are in a waiting season, we can remember that Christmas is a reminder that You are a God who keeps His promises. In Jesus's name, amen.

THINK

_____

_____

_____

PRAY

_____

_____

_____

PRAISE

_____

_____

_____

TO-DO   PRAYER LIST

_____   _____

_____   _____

_____   _____

QUESTIONS FOR DEEPER REFLECTION

1. When was a time you had to wait for something? How did you keep hoping?

_____

_____

_____

2. What did you learn about God while you waited?

_____

_____

_____

DAY 9

RISE AND SHINE

Arise, shine, for your light has come,
and the glory of the Lord has risen upon you.
—Isaiah 60:1

Have you ever been a little bit disappointed on Christmas Day? Maybe you hoped to spend your Christmas with family or friends, and it just didn't work out the way you planned. Or perhaps you made your Christmas list extra early with the expectation that a certain gift would be under the tree, but when you woke up on Christmas morning, the gift was nowhere to be found. I remember the first Christmas I was disappointed. The year was 1978, and there was one gift I wanted with every bit of my seven-year-old heart. I told Santa about it. I reminded my mom to tell Santa about it. I wrote letters. I had high expectations. I just *knew* that I was going to get that gift, and it would change my life.

When Christmas morning arrived, I was relieved to see *Mr. Microphone* under the tree. I took it out of the package, put the batteries in as directed, and tuned my FM radio to the correct station. But when I started to sing, my voice did not come through the radio as promised. My mom explained that it was broken; maybe it had fallen out of Santa's sleigh. I was devasted and my dreams of becoming a pop star died with that disappointment. All kidding aside, I know we'd sometimes rather stay in bed on Christmas morning than celebrate. Maybe we just need to remember not only the true meaning of Christmas, but our part in it as well.

SOMETHING TO THINK ABOUT

God's glory is serious business. When Moses asked God to show him His glory in Exodus 33:18–23, God hid Moses behind a rock and covered him with His hand. God only permitted Moses to see His back. Even so, Scripture tells us that when Moses came down the mountain, he shone with the residue of God's presence. (See Exodus 34:29.) I love that Moses asked to see God's glory and God protected him from that blinding light.

Today's key verse is a clarion call for us to wake up out of our sometimes disappointed and discouraged demeanors and remember that the light has come. God's glory is upon us like the dawn of a new day, transforming us from sleepers to wide-awake, joy-filled reflectors of His light. Just like Israel recognized God's glory on Moses, others should see Him in our lives as well. This Christmas, we have reason to celebrate no matter what is under the tree or who comes to Christmas breakfast.

Let's be the first to arise and give God the glory.

EXTRA VERSES FOR STUDY OR PRAYER

Exodus 33:18; Exodus 34:29; John 17:20–22

VERSE OF THE DAY

Arise, shine, for your light has come, and the glory of the LORD has risen upon you.   —Isaiah 60:1

PRAYER

Father, thank You for the glory You have given Jesus. You have extended that same glory to us because we are in Him, and He is in us. He prayed it would be true before He went to the cross. May we wake up today with a fresh desire to shine because Your light has come. In Jesus's name, amen.

THINK

PRAY

PRAISE

TO-DO

PRAYER LIST

QUESTIONS FOR DEEPER REFLECTION

1. What gift did you truly want as child that you didn't get? How did you handle that disappointment?

---

2. What does it look like for you today to be aware of the glory of God in your life and share it with others?

DAY 10

THE GIFT
I WANT MOST

He reveals deep and hidden things; he knows what is in the
darkness, and the light dwells with him.
—Daniel 2:22

In Scripture, light sometimes symbolizes knowledge and understanding. Light reveals and exposes. Nothing hides in the light. On the other hand, darkness communicates confusion and ignorance. It covers and conceals. In the light, we find comfort, while the darkness holds despair. Daniel knew this. He lived it. As a young Hebrew boy who was kidnapped and taken to Babylon to serve a foreign king, he faced this duality every single day. More importantly, Daniel knew who God was and how He embodied light. And when he needed wisdom and understanding, he prayed and asked God for help.

SOMETHING TO THINK ABOUT

When Daniel prayed to God, he first praised God. He honored God for having wisdom and power. He recognized that God was the one who changes the seasons and sets up kings and kingdoms. He declared that God gives wisdom to the wise and even greater knowledge to those who have understanding. And Daniel understood that God is the only One who has the power to reveal profound and hidden things. God even knows what the darkness is, even though He Himself is surrounded by light.

Daniel went on to thank God for giving him wisdom and power and answering his request. Why? Because the God who opens the depths did so for Daniel, and He solved the king's mystery—which was no mystery to God Himself.

I find it interesting that when Daniel told the king the meaning of his dream, he gave God all the glory. He didn't hold on to any of it for himself. Repeatedly, he pointed to God as the giver of all wisdom and revealer of dreams. And how did the king respond? He honored God and promoted Daniel:

> *Then King Nebuchadnezzar fell upon his face and paid homage to Daniel, and commanded that an offering and incense be offered up to him. The king answered and said to Daniel, "Truly, your God is God of gods and Lord of kings, and a revealer of mysteries, for you have been able to reveal this mystery." Then the king gave Daniel high honors and many great gifts and made him ruler over the whole province of Babylon and chief prefect over all the wise men of Babylon.* —Daniel 2:46–48

Friends, the older I get, the one gift I pray for more than anything else will not fit into a perfectly wrapped present under the tree. The gift I want most is wisdom. I want Him to enlighten my heart and give me understanding of His perfect will. I want clarity in dark times. I desire deep and hidden things to make sense and not feel heavy. I want the light and wisdom of God to ooze from my lips as I counsel women at my church, sit around dinner tables with my girlfriends, and pray over decisions my daughters are trying to make every day. I'm so grateful for this encouragement from Jesus, the light of the world:

> *Ask, and it will be given to you; seek, and you will find; knock, and it will be opened to you. For everyone who asks receives, and the one who seeks finds, and to the one who knocks it will be opened.* —Matthew 7:7–8

May it be so.

EXTRA VERSES FOR STUDY OR PRAYER

Psalm 139:11–12; Luke 12:2

VERSE OF THE DAY

He reveals deep and hidden things; he knows what is in the darkness, and the light dwells with him. —Daniel 2:22

PRAYER

Father, You are surrounded by light, full of wisdom and understanding. This Christmas, may we seek the gift of light-filled wisdom that is only found in You. And when You answer our prayers and give us this gift, we will be careful to give You all the glory. In Jesus's name, amen.

THINK

PRAY

PRAISE

TO-DO

PRAYER LIST

QUESTIONS FOR DEEPER REFLECTION

1. How would the gift of wisdom and understanding impact your life right now?

2. Write a prayer of only adoration and praise to God.

DAY 11

A NEW DAY DAWNING

And you, child, will be called the prophet of the Most High;
for you will go before the Lord to prepare his ways, to give
knowledge of salvation to his people in the forgiveness of their
sins, because of the tender mercy of our God,
whereby the sunrise shall visit us from on high to give light to
those who sit in darkness and in the shadow of death,
to guide our feet into the way of peace.
—Luke 1:76–79

Recently, I was gifted a weekend at a beach condo not too far from my house. Each morning of my visit, with quiet expectation, I made my way to the balcony to watch the sunrise. I sat with my legs curled up beneath me in my chair, cup of coffee in hand, and eyes wide open waiting for the first light to appear. This is one of my favorite things to do because I love watching the sun come up and seeing the colors dance on the water. I am always amazed at the certainty of the sunrise, especially at the ocean. Have you ever noticed how the light of morning always wins over the darkness and the sky responds to dawn without resistance?

And a new day's beginning is always packed with hope.

SOMETHING TO THINK ABOUT

Before the birth of Jesus came the birth of John the Baptist. He was the miracle child of a priest named Zechariah and his wife

Elizabeth. They were both advanced in years and without children. Scripture tells us that Elizabeth was barren. John's angelic birth announcement was shocking—so much so that Zechariah was struck mute by the angel Gabriel because he doubted it was possible. What loosened his tongue several months later at his son's birth was praise empowered by the Holy Spirit.

Zechariah foretold that John would prepare the way of the Lord and call God's people to turn from their sins. And as Zechariah poetically prophesied over his infant, he also spoke of Jesus, whom he likened to heaven's sunrise, the dayspring, giving light to the people who sat in darkness and despair. This was monumental for God's people because they had been waiting during four hundred years of prophetic silence—barren like Elizabeth—for God to speak to them. God was working while they were waiting, but the darkness felt heavy at times. John's birth signified heaven's first light was on His way. Zechariah's prophecy reminds me of this old hymn we sang when I was growing up:

SEND THE LIGHT

There's a call comes ringing o'er the restless wave,
"Send the light! Send the light!"
There are souls to rescue, there are souls to save,
Send the light! Send the light!

Send the light, the blessed gospel light;
Let it shine from shore to shore!
Send the light and let its radiant beams
Light the world forevermore![4]

By God's tender mercy, He sent the Light. His name was Jesus. And He was right on time.

---

4. Charles H. Gabriel, "Send the Light," 1888, library.timelesstruths.org/music/Send_the_ Light.

EXTRA VERSES FOR STUDY OR PRAYER
Job 38:12; 1 Peter 1:20

VERSE OF THE DAY

Because of the tender mercy of our God, whereby the sunrise shall visit us from on high. —Luke 1:78

PRAYER

Father, thank You that You are merciful and ready to help us in our darkness and despair. You didn't let the shadow of death win. You sent Your Son—the dayspring, heaven's first light, and the bright morning star—to show us the way of peace. O Lord, keep sending the light of the gospel to be born fresh in our hearts today and every day. In Jesus's name, amen.

THINK

PRAY

PRAISE

TO-DO

PRAYER LIST

QUESTIONS FOR DEEPER REFLECTION

1. Describe your favorite sunrise moment in detail. What do you see? What do you feel? How does light win every time?

----

2. Imagine how Zechariah must have felt to burst forth into praise after being mute for months. You can find his full prophetic song in Luke 1:68–79. What does his message express? How does he honor God?

DAY 12

NO ORDINARY NIGHT

*And in the same region there were shepherds
out in the field, keeping watch over their flock by night.
And an angel of the Lord appeared to them,
and the glory of the Lord shone around them, and they were
filled with great fear. And the angel said to them, "Fear not, for
behold, I bring you good news of great joy that will be for all
the people. For unto you is born this day in the city of David a
Savior, who is Christ the Lord."*
—Luke 2:8–11

I like to imagine the shepherds' night shift started like every other night. Maybe they herded the sheep into the fold, counted them, and divided up their night watch duties. They might have shared a meager meal and taken care of whatever needs their flock had at the time. Were any wounded? Did they need oil poured over their head to keep the bugs away? Had they grazed enough to be well fed for the night? Did they need water? Their flock probably settled in slowly and huddled close together for warmth. But not the shepherds. They were keepers of the flock. Awake and watchful. It was their job to keep the sheep safe from predators bent on destruction in the darkness. But this was no ordinary night—it was a miracle unfolding.

Suddenly light exploded all around them. It was as though night had suddenly become day. The source of this blinding light was an angel surrounded by the glory of the Lord—the very presence of God

Himself. Throughout Scripture, light is always associated with the presence of God because where God dwells, there is light.

What happens when a ragtag group of shepherds encounters the glory of God? They were immediately terror stricken. They couldn't hide. They couldn't run. They were paralyzed by fear. But not for long. The fierce and glory-shining angel told them not to fear because he was there to bring them good news of great joy. This good news, or gospel, was for all people—even shepherds on a hillside outside Bethlehem.

SOMETHING TO THINK ABOUT

In the ancient world, "gospel" meant an announcement of a new government. When a new king took over, messengers went throughout the land proclaiming the gospel or good news of the new ruler. So who was this new king? What was the good news being proclaimed to the shepherds? The angel went on to tell them that today in David's city, a baby had been born. But this is no ordinary baby. He was (and is):

+ A Savior

+ Who is Christ

+ The Lord

These three titles reveal the greatness of Jesus. And in this one light-filled sentence, His entire identity is declared: He is their deliverer, Messiah, and master of all. This baby is God. He had come on a rescue mission, and they were the first to know He had arrived. This baby, the Christ, would be the sacrificial Lamb who would take away their sins forever. Do you see why God announced this great news to the shepherds first? Nothing in Scripture is trivial. God is always in the details.

The angel issued an invitation for the shepherds to go and see. He told them exactly where they could find this miracle child. *"And this will be a sign for you: you will find a baby wrapped in swaddling cloths and lying in a manger"* (Luke 2:12). Their Messiah wasn't in a palace or a fine home.

He was in an unexpected place, wrapped in a threadbare garment, and lying in an animal trough. Many would have heard this and questioned it. But not these simple, unsophisticated shepherds. They ran to town to see the baby. They found him exactly as the messenger of God had said. He was everything they longed for and nothing like they expected.

Their response was extraordinary. They told everyone about what they had seen and all who heard the good news marveled at their testimony. When the shepherds went back to the fields to care for their sheep, they were glorifying and praising God. And they waited. But this time, they waited in the light, with hope, because of Jesus.

EXTRA VERSES FOR STUDY OR PRAYER

Micah 5:2; Luke 2:7; Luke 2:15–18

VERSE OF THE DAY

And an angel of the Lord appeared to them, and the glory of the Lord shone around them, and they were filled with great fear.
—Luke 2:9

PRAYER

Father, thank You for wrapping Your Son's birth announcement in light and delivering it to an unlikely group of shepherds. They didn't question the details. They ran to see the king. I pray this Christmas that my heart will be ready to receive the good news of Jesus with great joy. Help me to tell everyone I meet about my Savior, who is Christ the Lord, and all He has done for me. In Jesus's name, amen.

THINK

PRAY

_____

_____

_____

PRAISE

_____

_____

_____

TO-DO   PRAYER LIST

_____   _____

_____   _____

_____   _____

QUESTIONS FOR DEEPER REFLECTION

1. In the Bible, God seems to have a soft spot for shepherds. Can you think of other places in Scripture that refer to shepherds and what they do for their sheep?

_____

_____

_____

2. How does the shepherds' response to the glory of the Lord connect with what we have learned so far about the Light? What surprises you about this story?

_____

_____

_____

DAY 13

AT LAST

A light for revelation to the Gentiles,
and for glory to your people Israel.
—Luke 2:32

The word *advent* comes from the Latin word *adventus*, which means "to come."[5] If you follow the liturgical church calendar, you probably have some idea of how Advent is celebrated between Thanksgiving and Christmas. As I mentioned previously, my family has observed this season of expectation for over twenty years. It gives us a chance to build anticipation for Christmas while pausing to consider what it was like to wait for Jesus to come. One story that helps us understand what this meant to those who experienced it involves a man named Simeon, a promise, and a revelation that caused Jesus's parents to marvel at what was said about their son.

SOMETHING TO THINK ABOUT

We don't know much about this man named Simeon. Luke tells us he was a righteous man who carefully observed the Law of the Lord. He had a heart that was prayerful and expectant for the divine help that God would send to Israel. Luke also makes a point to tell us that the Holy Spirit was upon Simeon. This is significant because before the Holy Spirit came at Pentecost, God's Spirit was present but did not dwell continually within the hearts of God's children as

---

5. *Webster's Dictionary 1828*, s.v. "Advent," webstersdictionary1828.com/Dictionary/Advent.

a sign of His salvation. Instead, He came upon them and *acted* at different times for His glory. What happened in the temple that day was no coincidence. It was Spirit-led and Spirit-filled. You see, the Holy Spirit promised Simeon *"that he would not see death before he had seen the Lord's Christ"* (Luke 2:26) and He led Simeon to the temple that day. The Spirit identified the infant Jesus and prompted Simeon to take the child in his arms and bless God.

I love how the *New Living Translation* puts Simeon's words:

Sovereign Lord, now let your servant die in peace, as you have promised. I have seen your salvation, which you have prepared for all people. He is a light to reveal God to the nations, and he is the glory of your people Israel! —Luke 2:29–32 NLT

Simeon blessed God because He kept His promise to allow his servant to at last see His salvation. What Simeon says next is extraordinary. This help wasn't just for Israel—it was for all the nations of the world. *In Jesus, God revealed His light to everyone.* This would be a glory to Israel because the Messiah came *through them for the entire world.*

Can you imagine what that moment was like? Do you suspect, as I do, that Simeon had tears of joy as he spoke? Do you wonder if Joseph and Mary looked at each other to make sure they were both hearing the same thing? Luke tells us that they *"marveled at what was said about him"* (Luke 2:33). Simeon blessed them and told Mary that the mission of her child would bring the rise and fall of many in Israel, He would be misunderstood, and a sword would pierce her soul as well. The coming of the long-awaited Messiah brought a beautiful blessing and brutal honesty from a prayerful prophet who had held God's promise in his humble arms.

Bless the Lord, oh my soul, for I have seen Your salvation.

EXTRA VERSES FOR STUDY OR PRAYER

Luke 10:21; Colossians 2:3

VERSE OF THE DAY

A light for revelation to the Gentiles, and for glory to your people Israel. —Luke 2:32

PRAYER

Father, thank You that You sent Your salvation for everyone. This Advent, may I be prayerfully expectant like Simeon, knowing that You always keep Your light-filled promises. In Jesus's name, amen.

THINK

PRAY

PRAISE

TO-DO

PRAYER LIST

QUESTIONS FOR DEEPER REFLECTION

1. What has God promised you?

_____

_____

_____

2. How are you praying with an expectant heart?

_____

_____

_____

DAY 14

WHEN YOU THINK THE DARKNESS MAY WIN

In him was life, and the life was the light of men. The light shines in the darkness, and the darkness has not overcome it.
—John 1:4–5

A few years ago, suddenly and unexpectedly, we had to move out of our house of more than thirteen years. Not only did we move, but we also downsized by half a house. Our much smaller home was now bursting at the seams. Don't get me wrong, we were grateful to have a soft place to land, but by the time Christmas rolled around, I was tired of trying to see the bright side of our tiny home.

One problem we encountered was that our artificial *Martha Stewart Pre-Lit Christmas Tree* did not fit with our home's lower ceilings. I loved that gorgeous, fluffy, tall tree. It stood witness to so many family memories over the years. But there was no space for it. And so, we donated it and started considering other options as Christmas drew near. This was made more difficult by having an even tinier budget. We didn't have the money to buy a new tree, artificial or otherwise. My girls were worried that this would be the worst Christmas ever. I was praying that wouldn't be the case, but honestly, I wasn't sure how God was going to work it all out. I thought maybe this would be the year that darkness won over the light.

Imagine my surprise when my daughter Emma called me and said, "Mom, send Dad with the van to pick me up at work. I have a Christmas tree for us!" As it turned out, there was a Christmas shop next door to the bakery where she was working. Every season, the Christmas store discarded last year's must-have Christmas decorations because they weren't this year's must-have Christmas decorations. And by discarded, I mean they tossed them in a dumpster. When my daughter went outside to toss something in the same dumpster, she was shocked to see a full-size Christmas tree that had gone from a festive floor display to garbage in one afternoon. She had no shame in rescuing that Christmas tree. In fact, her coworker helped her, and she did it with great joy. And guess what? That dumpster Christmas tree fit perfectly in our living room.

SOMETHING TO THINK ABOUT

When John tells us the Christmas story, he takes us back. Not to the Gabriel announcement or the straw-strewn stable birth of the Christ child. John flies us back to the split second before creation to show us that God was already dwelling with the Word—who was life and light. In John 1:1–5, he then retells the creation story with the Word as eternally present and central to the story.

- The Word was *with* God.
- The Word *was* God.
- The Word breathed *life* into all things.
- And this life was a *light* shining for everyone.

This light thrived in the darkness even though the darkness tried to overcome it. No matter how the darkness tried to extinguish it, the Light could not be stopped. Do you need evidence of that? Look to the birth of Jesus. The Word made flesh is now life and light dwelling among us.

Christmas was hard that year we put up a tree that had been tossed in a dumpster. But every morning in December, after I turned on the Christmas tree lights, I grabbed my favorite coffee mug filled with a dark roast brew and sat down to consider the Word made flesh. I was reminded that the Light always wins.

EXTRA VERSES FOR STUDY OR PRAYER

John 14:1; John 20:31; Hebrews 4:12

VERSE OF THE DAY

In him was life, and the life was the light of men. The light shines in the darkness, and the darkness has not overcome it.

—John 1:4–5

PRAYER

Father, I love the reminder that the light thrives in the darkness and the darkness never wins. Thank You that the Word was with You in the beginning and breathes life and light into my heart every day. In Jesus's name, amen.

THINK

PRAY

PRAISE

TO-DO

PRAYER LIST

QUESTIONS FOR DEEPER REFLECTION

1. How does John's perspective on the Word made flesh encourage your heart?

2. Make a list today of all the ways the Light is overcoming the darkness.

DAY 15

THE TRUE
LIGHT SHINES

The true light, which gives light to everyone,
was coming into the world.
—John 1:9

The school my girls attend has a sweet tradition. When they graduate, their parents walk across the stage, meet them halfway, and present them with their diploma. I've now done this three separate times, and I can't tell you how hard I pray I can physically walk across the stage. I must fight back a flood of tears (often unsuccessfully) and the incredible lump in my throat as the school shows pictures from the students' first day of kindergarten. I try to be so cool in that moment and I fail every time. Well, it's true what they say: babies don't keep. And kids grow up to take their place in the world even if we aren't ready for it to happen.

SOMETHING TO THINK ABOUT

Remember the baby named John we met a couple of days ago? I love that profound and precious moment with his parents, who are filled with hope and joy. I think they were proud of their son and a little bit in awe of what his life would mean. Maybe they didn't want him to grow up just yet. I can understand that perfectly well. But guess what? That baby grew up and took his place in the world.

Another John picked up John the Baptist's story in chapter 1 of his gospel account. He said:

> *He came as a witness, to bear witness about the light, that all might believe through him. He was not the light but came to bear witness about the light.* —John 1:7–8

John the Baptist's special mission was that he was sent by God as a witness to the light. The words his father proclaimed over him came true. John told everyone about the Light. He prepared the way. He made sure everyone knew *he* wasn't the light, but he showed everyone where to look and who to believe in.

Who did John point to? He pointed people to Jesus, who is the one true Light. Jesus entered our world, a world He made (light and all), and shined His true light upon the heart of everyone. This Jesus was blazingly beautiful but not everyone thought so. They didn't recognize Him, let alone believe in Him. Some just plain refused to listen. Others didn't receive Him as the true Light. Maybe the mystery was just too hard for them to comprehend. Perhaps they were looking for an altogether different kind of light. Or maybe they weren't looking for light at all.

One thing I can't quite get over is the fact that Jesus didn't shine light from far away. He bridged the distance and brought His true Light near. He took on flesh and shone His Light so we could experience it for ourselves. And the sweetest part for us who believe is that when we place our trust in Him, we are completely reborn as children of God.

We can bear witness to the true Light too. We do this when we prepare the way through relationships with our neighbors or tell people at work about Jesus. And yes, we bear witness to the Light when we raise our kids with truth, praying they will one day trust in Him as well. I know that being a witness to the Light can be intimidating at times. But Christmas provides an amazing opportunity to point to Jesus and see what happens. You just never know when the true Light will shine on a heart, and they will believe.

EXTRA VERSES FOR STUDY OR PRAYER

Matthew 3:1; John 1:14; 1 John 2:8

VERSE OF THE DAY

The true light, which gives light to everyone, was coming into the world. —John 1:9

PRAYER

Father, You sent Jesus as the true Light that would shine on everyone. He became man for us to experience Him up close and personally. May we, like John the Baptist, tell everyone we know about Jesus and how they can know the true Light themselves. Help us at Christmas to have an extra measure of boldness as we point others to You. In Jesus's name, amen.

THINK

PRAY

PRAISE

TO-DO

PRAYER LIST

QUESTIONS FOR DEEPER REFLECTION

1. How does John prepare the way for the true Light?

2. What is different about your life now that you know the true Light? How does He fill your heart and reflect in your life to others?

3. What is one way you can tell others about the true Light?

DAY 16

WHAT THE PEOPLE LOVED MORE THAN LIGHT

And this is the judgment: the light has come into the world, and people loved the darkness rather than the light because their works were evil.
—John 3:19

My family loves a good Christmas movie. We start on Thanksgiving with *White Christmas* and work our way joyously through December with one hope-filled story after another. If your family is like mine, you have a similar list as well. I don't think I'm going out on a limb here too much, but if I said, "Bah humbug," you would know without a doubt what story I was talking about. The character of Ebenezer Scrooge stands as one of the greatest redemption stories of all time. He went from Christmas curmudgeon to Saint Nick quicker than Tiny Tim could say, "God bless us every one!" It only took three ghosts and a good look at the emptiness his current path would lead to in the end. If only every story had a happy ending, and hearts really did grow three times larger when given the opportunity.

SOMETHING TO THINK ABOUT

As much we love a good redemption story, Jesus warned us that not every story would end that way. In his conversation with Nicodemus in John 3, Jesus tells him good news but doesn't mince words about the bad. He says God loved the world so much He sent His Son so that no one would have to die without Him but would instead have eternal life. God sent Jesus not to condemn the world, but to save it. What does it take to be saved? We simply need to believe in the One God sent.

Yet just as at creation when God said, *"Let there be light"* and the physical boundary lines were drawn, when God sent Jesus—the true Light—into the world, a spiritual boundary line was drawn. Darkness fled, and the people who loved the dark fled too. In some ways, it is unimaginable to think that there are people who prefer their pride more than the light. They cherish their sin more than freedom. And they hate the light because it exposes their destructive deeds—deeds they would rather hide and hold on to than walk with God in the light.

Does this break your heart like it does mine? I think in the middle of this season of Christmas, we should take some time to pray for those around us who need the love and light of Christ to flood their lives. I can imagine that you know at least one person who needs this type of intercessory prayer today. I have found people tend to be more open to the Gospel message at Christmastime than any other time of year. Perhaps this will be the year their hearts will receive the good news that love was born at Christmas. And that light still shines.

EXTRA VERSES FOR STUDY OR PRAYER

Ephesians 3:14–19; Revelation 3:20

VERSE OF THE DAY

And this is the judgment: the light has come into the world, and people loved the darkness rather than the light because their works were evil.   —John 3:19

PRAYER

Father, You sent Your Son into the world because You loved us and desired to have an eternal relationship with us. That is the best news. I know people right now who don't know You personally. They live in darkness. I pray that You would knock on the door of their hearts today. Open their eyes, Lord, to the Light and love You have for them. In Jesus's name, amen.

THINK

PRAY

PRAISE

TO-DO

PRAYER LIST

QUESTIONS FOR DEEPER REFLECTION

1. When did you first understand that God sent His Son Jesus because He loved you and wanted to save you?

    _____

    _____

    _____

2. Make a list of people who don't know Jesus and pray for them every day until Christmas. Ask God to bring them to salvation.

    _____

    _____

    _____

THE LIGHT OF THE WORLD HAS COME

Again Jesus spoke to them, saying,
"I am the light of the world.
Whoever follows me will not walk in darkness,
but will have the light of life."
—John 8:12

Several years ago, I made a commitment to read the entire Bible in ninety days. It took about one hour of dedicated reading each day. I started on Memorial Day and finished around Labor Day with a couple days off thrown in as a buffer. I noticed as I read that the Old Testament had a distinct pattern. God would reveal His character and pursue relationship with His people. They would respond and say, "Yes," but after a time, they would turn back to idols and worship other gods. This resulted in consequences that they had been warned about. Then God would woo them back, they would once again respond, and the cycle would start all over again. It felt like an uphill battle. But once I started the New Testament and Jesus came, everything changed. Suddenly there were no barriers between God and His people to know Him, and they were empowered by His Spirit to walk with Him. When the Light burst onto the scene, the pace of the story flew by at warp speed. It was as if I blinked and found myself on the final page of Revelation, crying my eyes out.

SOMETHING TO THINK ABOUT

As we have followed the theme of light through Scripture, it has felt a little bit like my full read through the Bible so many years ago. But the good news is that everything we have learned about light up until now points to Jesus. I love how Lysa TerKeurst put it: "Jesus in every way fulfills and surpasses every image and symbol of light that came before Him."[6] Jesus is the Light of the world. Today's passage tells us that Jesus knew who He was and what He came to do. When Jesus enters this scene at the Feast of Tabernacles (see John 7), there had already been a glorious celebration with water and light as the key elements for several days. Every night, the priests would light large candle stands that stood on the top of the temple. The extraordinary physical light display symbolized the pillar of fire the Israelites followed in the desert. It reminded them of God's presence with them in the wilderness but also pointed to the coming Messiah. When Jesus declared, *I am the light of world* in the midst of this festival of light, He was saying, "The Light has come."

He also made two promises. First, He said when you follow Him, you will not walk in darkness. This does not mean there will not be darkness in our world. We have clearly established that darkness exists. But as followers of the Light, we will never be alone. Second, Jesus promised that when we follow Him, we will have the *light of life.* This kind of life is genuine, blessed, and flourishing because we have constant access to the Light of the world. It is through our relationship with Jesus that we experience true life and light. Oh, friend, keep walking with the Light of the world. He promised us the blessed life is with Him.

The best is yet to come.

EXTRA VERSES FOR STUDY OR PRAYER

John 7:14–18; Ephesians 4:1; 1 Peter 2:9

---

6. Lysa TerKeurst, *Finding I AM: How Jesus Fully Satisfies the Cry of Your Heart* (Nashville, TN: Lifeway, 2016), 49.

VERSE OF THE DAY

Again Jesus spoke to them, saying, "I am the light of the world. Whoever follows me will not walk in darkness, but will have the light of life." —John 8:12

PRAYER

Father, thank You that You sent Jesus to be the true Light of the world. We believe that when we walk with Him, we will never walk alone, and we will have true life in Him. Thank You for these precious promises. May we walk worthy of Him in all that we say and do. In Jesus's name, amen.

THINK

PRAY

PRAISE

TO-DO

PRAYER LIST

QUESTIONS FOR DEEPER REFLECTION

1. What is your impression of our study of the Light so far?

----

2. What is one way Jesus fulfills the image of light?

----

3. Which promises from John 8:12 mean the most to you right now? Why?

DAY 18

BELIEVE IN THE LIGHT

While you have the light, believe in the light,
that you may become sons of light.
—John 12:36

My favorite night of the year is the candlelight service at my church on Christmas Eve. The tagline for the service is "Night of 4,000 Lights." This is no lie because my church worship center is massive, and on Christmas Eve, every seat is filled—and then some. After we sing and the Christmas story is shared, our senior pastor starts with one candle, and he passes the light to another person. Soon it is passed to the entire room. Once every candle is lit, we sing "Silent Night" and raise our candles higher with each stanza until our hands are raised high and the light fills the room. Even with many near misses, dripping wax, and stressed-out parents of little ones, it is one of the most beautiful representations of what happens when the light is received, passed, and multiplied.

SOMETHING TO THINK ABOUT

In John 11, Jesus raises His good friend Lazarus from the dead. This miracle rocked the local community and set into motion (rather quickly) the events that would ultimately lead to Jesus's own death on the cross and His resurrection three days later. It is within this immediate context that we find Jesus teaching and calling the crowds to believe in Him.

> *So Jesus said to them, "The light is among you for a little while longer. Walk while you have the light, lest darkness overtake you. The one who walks in the darkness does not know where he is going. **While you have the light, believe in the light, that you may become sons of light.**"*   —John 12:35–36

Jesus knew His time was short. And He urged the crowds to put their faith in Him before it was too late. His invitation comes with this assurance: When you believe in the Light, you yourself will become children of light. As children of light, you will have the Light of Christ within you, and His light will shine through you.

Just like on Christmas Eve when four thousand candles are lit and held high, as followers of Jesus, we carry His light with us wherever we go. And sometimes at Christmas, when our hearts are stirred to believe more, our lights shine a little brighter. And we'll sing that old gospel tune, "This little light of mine, I'm going to let it shine…"

EXTRA VERSES FOR STUDY OR PRAYER

Matthew 21:22; John 11:9; Hebrews 11:6

VERSE OF THE DAY

While you have the light, believe in the light, that you may become sons of light.   —John 12:36

PRAYER

Father, thank You that You give us the right to become Your children when we believe in the Light. May we always be aware that as children of light, we carry the Light of Jesus everywhere we go. In Jesus's name, amen.

THINK

PRAY

PRAISE

TO-DO

PRAYER LIST

QUESTIONS FOR DEEPER REFLECTION

1. Does your family typically attend any special Christmas services at church? What is it about this time of worship that encourages your heart?

2. How do you stir up your belief during this Christmas season?

3. How can you carry the Light of Jesus with you today?

DAY 19

JESUS CAME AS THE LIGHT

I have come into the world as light, so that whoever believes in me may not remain in darkness.
—John 12:46

We drove "home" for Christmas only once. The year after our big move to Florida, we packed up our van with warm winter clothes, Christmas presents, baby gear, and lots of snacks before heading north. I had been homesick and missing my family and the annual Christmas traditions that surrounded the season. About four hours from my parents' house, it started to snow. And rain. And then freezing rain. And more snow. As this winter mix worsened, I imagined that we would be forced to spend our Christmas (if we were fortunate) in a Motel 6 just off the interstate and miles from happy Christmas memories waiting to wrap us up.

I'm not sure how we made it through that mess. Most likely it was a combination of my mom's prayers and my husband's patient determination to get us there. But hours past our intended arrival, we pulled into the snow-stacked driveway, scooped up our girls, and headed toward the light in the window. We were immediately welcomed with warm hugs from my mom and dad. At which point, I promptly burst into tears.

We stayed for a week and drove back to Florida in much better conditions. When we arrived back at our home in Florida, I said to my husband, "I will never ask you to do that again." I wanted my old-fashioned Indiana family Christmas and my new Florida family all in one place. But I realized in that moment that I couldn't have it both ways. And for the last twenty years, during the Christmas season, we have filled our own Florida home with light and life and all Jesus brings.

SOMETHING TO THINK ABOUT

In Jesus's last public sermon, He boldly spoke about light. But He didn't say this quietly. In fact, a couple of verses before our verse of the day, we read, "And Jesus cried out and said, 'Whoever believes in me, believes not in me but in him who sent me'" (John 12:44). He delivered this final message in earnest. He was pleading loudly with the people to believe in Him. He was giving them a choice. Did they believe His message or not? He was offering one last chance for them to believe in Him.

As if to provide further evidence, Jesus goes on to say that He came into the world "as light." Did you catch that? He didn't become light; He existed as light before He came. Hebrews 13:8 reminds us, "Jesus Christ is the same yesterday and today and forever." This means that He was light before He took on human flesh, He was the Light of the world while He was here, and He will be light in the new heaven and the new earth. This amazing truth is followed by the tender promise that whoever believes in Him will be delivered from darkness. Jesus came to displace the darkness and rescue those who believe in Him. And in the end, we have a choice: Light forever with Jesus or darkness.

I'll choose the Light.

EXTRA VERSES FOR STUDY OR PRAYER

Joshua 24:14–15; Hebrews 13:8; James 1:17

VERSE OF THE DAY

I have come into the world as light, so that whoever believes in me may not remain in darkness. —John 12:46

PRAYER

Father, thank You that Jesus came as the light. He didn't need to become light because Light was truly who He was. And because He was the Light, is the Light, and will always be the Light, we don't have to remain in the darkness. With Jesus, we have all the Light we need to live every day. In Jesus's name, amen.

THINK

PRAY

PRAISE

TO-DO

PRAYER LIST

QUESTIONS FOR DEEPER REFLECTION

1. What does it mean for you when you realize that Jesus's last public message was about light?

    _____

    _____

    _____

2. Why do you think Jesus *"cried out"* His final sermon with so much passion?

    _____

    _____

    _____

DAY 20

THE DAY THE
WORLD WENT DARK

*It was now about the sixth hour, and there was darkness over
the whole land until the ninth hour, while the sun's light failed.
And the curtain of the temple was torn in two. Then Jesus,
calling out with a loud voice, said, "Father, into your hands I
commit my spirit!" And having said this he breathed his last.*
—Luke 23:44–46

Christmas music is my favorite genre. I think we need more time to hear it besides the weeks between Thanksgiving and Christmas. Though I'm a firm believer in Christmas decorations living their best life for only four weeks or so, the music of Christmas is divine and deserves more time to be enjoyed. When I am making my daily grocery store run, I love to hear music playing and Jesus's name being sung. I always smile and think, "God's going to use that in someone's life." Quite frankly, that person is usually me. The sounds of the season fill my heart to the full.

Although I will sing "Joy to the World" loudly at any time, my favorite Christmas songs are more contemplative and melancholy. They make me pause, pray, and consider how much God's people longed for Jesus to come. At the same time, they reveal a secret sadness that so many missed Him when He showed up in a way that they had not expected. When you consider that the moment Jesus was born, the timetable was set in motion for the day that darkness would cover the whole earth, these somber words and tunes with sharp notes make so much sense.

SOMETHING TO THINK ABOUT

What happened when the Light of the world was extinguished? Luke 23:44–45 tells us that for three hours, the sunlight failed. There was a total blackout. Some scientists believe there was a total eclipse of the sun on the day that Jesus was crucified.

In the spring of 2024, everyone in the United States was enamored with a solar eclipse. It had been a few years since an eclipse of this magnitude was visible in any part of the United States. Before that, it had been almost a hundred years since the previous eclipse. Those who were in the narrow path of totality—when the moon passes between the earth and the sun and blocks out the sun's rays entirely—described the event as spiritual. There was a sudden drop in temperature, a shift in the wind, and an eerie silence because birds and animals were confused, thinking it was night. Those with homemade solar viewers were in awe. How could they not be?

When Jesus died, people were deeply moved. And as the sun went dark, a couple of things happened. The curtain in the temple was torn in two from top to bottom. This curtain separated the holiest place in the temple, the place God's presence dwelled, from the outer courts. This was no coincidence. Jesus's death opened the way for all of us to come to God through forgiveness of sins. Many who had gathered to witness the crucifixion left beating their chests as a sign of grief. All but one. A Roman centurion praised God and declared, *"Certainly this man was innocent!"* (Luke 23:47).

I think it is fitting that the Creator of the universe would initiate such darkness at the death of His Son. It was as if Earth itself was weeping. And when we sing these lyrics at Christmas connecting His birth to His death, we mourn in our own way too:

O come, Thou Day-Spring, come and cheer
Our spirits by Thine Advent here;

Disperse the gloomy clouds of night,
And death's dark shadows put to flight.
Rejoice! Rejoice! Emmanuel
Shall come to thee, O Israel.[7]

Rejoice! Emmanuel has come.

EXTRA VERSES FOR STUDY OR PRAYER

Isaiah 7:14; Mark 15:33; Luke 19:10; John 19:30

VERSE OF THE DAY

It was now about the sixth hour, and there was darkness over the whole land until the ninth hour, while the sun's light failed. And the curtain of the temple was torn in two.   —Luke 22:44–45

PRAYER

Father, thank You for moments this Christmas season when I can pause and remember the real reason Your Son came as a baby at Christmas was to seek and save the lost. Jesus came to die on the cross for our sins. The day the world went dark was veiled in sadness, but hope would soon rise. And for that, we are so grateful today. In Jesus's name, amen.

THINK

7. William Henry Monk, *Hymns, Ancient and Modern, for Use in the Services of the Church* (London: J. Alfred Novello, 1861), 64.

PRAY

_____

_____

_____

PRAISE

_____

_____

_____

TO-DO

_____

_____

_____

PRAYER LIST

_____

_____

_____

QUESTIONS FOR DEEPER REFLECTION

1. What is your favorite Christmas song?

_____

_____

_____

2. Write down your favorite verse and turn it into a prayer back to the Lord.

_____

_____

_____

DAY 21

A CITY ON A HILL

You are the light of the world.
A city set on a hill cannot be hidden.
Nor do people light a lamp and put it under a basket,
but on a stand, and it gives light to all in the house.
—Matthew 5:14–15

The centerpiece of our family's Advent wreath is a large white pillar candle. This candle is called *the Christ candle* and it is only lit on Christmas Eve to mark the birth of Jesus. Every year, I buy four new taper candles to place in a circle around our Christ candle. I light them individually for the four weeks leading up to Christmas, adding a new candle each week. They burn low throughout the month as we draw closer to Christmas Eve. But our Christ candle is special. Because it is only lit for a few hours each year, I have used the same one for the past twenty-two years. And every year, as I carefully wrap and store it to make sure it will be kept safe for our next Christmas season, I thank God for the light it has given our house over the years and what it means for our family.

SOMETHING TO THINK ABOUT

As Jesus's ministry began to build momentum and the crowds increased, He took time to intentionally teach His closest disciples. He spoke directly to them and used the powerful metaphor of light to compare their significant presence in the world. He said that they were the light of the world. Their light would stand out because of their relationship with Him.

Light illuminates. It is not hidden under a basket. On the contrary, a light in a regular house would be set on a stand, in a prime location, to give enough light for the entire household to benefit. Jesus's disciples were to be just like that. They were to be lit from within and live public lives that would shine in a dark, dark world. Jesus told them, *"In the same way, let your light shine before others, so that they may see your good works and give glory to your Father who is in heaven"* (Matthew 5:16).

Lighting the Christ candle every Christmas Eve is a reminder to my family that Jesus came as the Light of the world. We don't hide the candle in a box. We take it out. We put it on display and enjoy the light that is and was and is to come. Our task as His followers is to keep bringing His light to the world—all for Jesus and the glory of our Father in heaven.

EXTRA VERSES FOR STUDY OR PRAYER

Matthew 5:1; John 8:12; John 9:5

VERSE OF THE DAY

You are the light of the world. A city set on a hill cannot be hidden.   —Matthew 5:14

PRAYER

Father, thank You for the reminder that as Your followers, we are not to live hidden lives. We are to shine because of our relationship with Your Son, the Light of the world. Remind us that it is virtually impossible for a city set on a hill to remain hidden. May we grasp our purpose today with a newfound commitment to shine brightly for You. In Jesus's name, amen.

THINK

PRAY

PRAISE

TO-DO

PRAYER LIST

QUESTIONS FOR DEEPER REFLECTION

1. Light a candle in an otherwise dark room sometime this week as a part of your Christmas celebration. What do you notice? How does the light fill the room?

----

2. How are you serving as a city on a hill in your community this Christmas?

_____

_____

_____

DAY 22

TURNING FROM DARKNESS TO LIGHT

*To open their eyes, so that they may turn
from darkness to light and from the power of Satan to God,
that they may receive forgiveness of sins and a place among
those who are sanctified by faith in me.*
—Acts 26:18

When my girls were little, I started reading aloud to them on an almost daily basis. I continued this until most of them went to high school. It was common to find us several mornings each week lounging on the couches or chairs, with them eating breakfast and me drinking a cup of coffee. During the Christmas season, we would gravitate toward stories we loved and wanted to revisit because they felt like old friends. One story we laughed and cried our way through from beginning to end was *The Best Christmas Pageant Ever.*[8] If you aren't familiar with this book, it is the story of a church's annual Christmas pageant and how one ragtag family of kids known for their less than holy behavior took over the entire production. By the end of the book, you love the Herdmans so much that you cheer wildly for them when they botch up their lines and stumble through the birth of Jesus. You can't help but see the nativity scene with fresh eyes (filled with tears) at their honest response to the gospel story come to life.

---

8. Barbara Robinson, *The Best Christmas Pageant Ever* (New York: Trumpet Club, 1972).

SOMETHING TO THINK ABOUT

Jesus was not your typical rabbi. He made a point to seek out the outcast, go to regions that were filled with gentiles like Samaria, and even heal on the Sabbath. He caused quite a stir with the typical religious folks of His day who wanted things done according to their traditions. He also made it clear that He *"came to seek and to save the lost"* (Luke 19:10) and that included a world that looked like the Herdmans.

In Acts 9, we meet a Pharisee named Saul who has a life-changing encounter with the Light of the world on his way to Damascus to kill followers of Jesus. Later, in telling the story of his conversion, he described the Light as shining brighter than the sun, and it caused him to crumble to the ground. From within the Light, he heard a voice saying, *"Saul, Saul, why are you persecuting me?"* (Acts 26:14) When Saul asked who he is speaking to, the response from the Light was, *"I am Jesus whom you are persecuting"* (verse 15).

Paul, temporarily blinded, is given a new mission by Jesus to go and preach the gospel to the gentiles. I love how Jesus describes it when He tells Saul—whose name becomes Paul—that he is being sent to testify of what he has seen *"to open their eyes, so that they may turn from darkness to light and from the power of Satan to God, that they may receive forgiveness of sins and a place among those who are sanctified by faith in me'"* (Acts 26:18). Paul obeys (how could he not?) and carries the light to the gentiles just like Jesus said he would.

This Christmas, wouldn't it be amazing to witness people turning from the darkness to the light? They might just slip or stumble into your Christmas Eve service. Maybe they will not look like you or dress like you. Maybe their kids will be noisy and run up and down the aisles. But maybe, just maybe, their eyes (and yours) will be opened to the Light of the world in the most extraordinary way.

EXTRA VERSES FOR STUDY OR PRAYER

Acts 9:1–9; Acts 9:17–19; Romans 1:1

VERSE OF THE DAY

To open their eyes, so that they may turn from darkness to light and from the power of Satan to God, that they may receive forgiveness of sins and a place among those who are sanctified by faith in me. —Acts 26:18

PRAYER

Father, thank You that You still open eyes, turn people's hearts from darkness to light, forgive sinners, and set us apart for Your holy purpose. May we, like Paul, say yes to You with our whole hearts. In Jesus's name, amen.

THINK

PRAY

PRAISE

TO-DO

PRAYER LIST

QUESTIONS FOR DEEPER REFLECTION

1. Do you find that people are more open to the gospel at Christmastime than at other times of the year? Why or why not?

2. How has encountering Jesus, the Light of the world, changed you?

DAY 23

THE
ARMOR OF LIGHT

The night is far gone; the day is at hand.
So then let us cast off the works of darkness
and put on the armor of light.
—Romans 13:12

There is a famous story from World War I called "The Christmas Truce of 1914." In this account, verified on both sides by German and British soldiers, opposing forces met in *no man's land* to celebrate Christmas.

> Normally, the British and Germans communicated across No Man's Land with streaking bullets, with only occasional gentlemanly allowances to collect the dead unmolested. But now, there were handshakes and words of kindness. The soldiers traded songs, tobacco and wine, joining in a spontaneous holiday party in the cold night.[9]

It is estimated that as many as 100,000 soldiers participated in this spontaneous, unsanctioned ceasefire. How do men go from shooting each other one minute to exchanging handshakes and gifts the next? No one is certain. But those who lived it were never the same.

---

9. A. J. Baime and Volker Janssen, "WWI's Christmas Truce: When Fighting Paused for the Holiday," updated April 15, 2025, www.history.com/articles/christmas-truce-1914-world-war-i-soldier-accounts.

SOMETHING TO THINK ABOUT

It is bittersweet to imagine a wartime truce on Christmas Eve. But the reality for Christ followers is that we are still very much in a battle between darkness and light. While the battle rages, we are called to live out our ordinary lives in extraordinary ways that honor God. How do we manage to do that? In today's key passage, Paul reminds us to cast off the works of darkness and put on the armor of light. We do this by fleeing from sin that easily entangles us and by avoiding dark patterns that lead us into sin. Some of the sins Paul tells us to avoid in Romans 13:13 are obvious ones like sexual immorality and drunkenness, but he also says to cast off quarreling and jealousy. Honestly, these seem to rear their ugly heads quite frequently during the Christmas season. Have you ever seen people fighting in a store over low stock of a must-have toy of the season? (Do you remember the frenzies over Cabbage Patch Kids, Beanie Babies, or Tickle Me Elmo?) The bottom line is that we need to get rid of anything and everything that doesn't look like Jesus.

Instead, we are to *put on the armor of light*" because the day of salvation is drawing near. This is such good news! The night may feel like it is growing darker, but the light is approaching, my friend. And we need to be ready. The word used here for *"put on"* is *endyō*, which means "to sink into clothing."[10] According to Romans 13:14, this means that we are to wrap or clothe ourselves with the Lord Jesus Christ.

Does this remind you of day 6, when we read about God covering Himself *"with light as with a garment, stretching out the heavens like a tent"* (Psalm 104:2)? The beauty we discover here is that because of Jesus, we are wrapped in His light as well. This light is not merely a heavenly garment. It is also the daily armor we wear and a constant protection in the heat of the battle against the darkness—not only during Christmas, but every day of the year.

EXTRA VERSES FOR STUDY OR PRAYER

Psalm 104:1–2; Ephesians 6:11, 13–18; Hebrews 10:25

---

10. G1746. *endyō. Strong's Greek Concordance.*

VERSE OF THE DAY

The night is far gone; the day is at hand. So then let us cast off the works of darkness and put on the armor of light.

—Romans 13:12

PRAYER

Father, it is a good reminder that the day is drawing near when Jesus will return. May we let go of sins that easily entangle us and instead sink into the armor of light that we wear because we are Your children. In Jesus's name, amen.

THINK

PRAY

PRAISE

TO-DO

PRAYER LIST

QUESTIONS FOR DEEPER REFLECTION

1. Is there a sin that easily entangles you especially this time of year? Be honest with the Lord through prayer and repentance. Ask Him to give you strength to flee from that scheme of the enemy to trip you up.

----

2. According to Ephesians 6:13–18, what are the individual pieces of the armor of God that we are to *"put on"* like clothing?

DAY 24

O CHRISTMAS CRATE

For God, who said,
"Let light shine out of darkness,"
has shone in our hearts to give the light of
the knowledge of the glory of God in the face of Jesus Christ.
But we have this treasure in jars of clay, to show that
the surpassing power belongs to God and not to us.
—2 Corinthians 4:6–7

It's true, we didn't have much. We were two broke college students living in a two-bedroom apartment. I met my roommate Robin during my freshman year at Indiana University when I showed up to her Bible study with Mary, a girl who lived on my dorm floor. Robin and I hit it off immediately and were ecstatic when it worked out for us to share an apartment our senior year. We grocery shopped together, cooked crockpot meals, ate brownies before they were completely cooled, and talked about Jesus. And boys. But mostly Jesus.

During our December finals week, we decided we needed a bit of Christmas cheer and a distraction from studying, but neither of us had the money to get a tree. Instead, we bought a cheap set of Christmas lights and covered the makeshift television stand we had made from an old moving crate. I'm not sure who started the song, but by the time we finished hanging the lights, "O Christmas Crate" was born. We left the lights up well past Christmas because we couldn't think of a single reason to take them down. The Christmas crate became the New Year's crate and then the Valentine's crate and so on. And just so you know, my mom still has the Christmas crate in her kitchen. And every time I see it, I can't help but smile and sing.

SOMETHING TO THINK ABOUT

I don't know why God chose sinful, broken people to be the place His glory Light dwells. But Scripture tells us that the same God who spoke light into existence is the same God who makes His home in our hearts. He sheds His light on the knowledge of God's glory that is revealed in the face of Christ. And now, in a stunning turn of events, this same light shines in and through us. All because of Jesus.

But wait. Most days, I feel less like a glorious Douglas fir from the forests of Oregon and more like a moving crate strung with lights—or, to borrow from our verse of the day, a fragile clay pot. Corinth was renowned for its pottery, so clay pots were readily available and used every day. They were common and practical and could be purchased at the market, but they cracked easily. But even in their fragile, common, cracked state, they could still be filled with oil to light a lamp that could brighten the whole house.

Why does God choose sinful, broken people to be lit from within by the power of His presence? Perhaps—and this is what Paul hints at here—it is because when we are weak, others can't help but see that the power is from God and not us. And when people see this, they might say, "I don't know how you do what you are doing," or "How did you survive that trial?" or "Why do you have so much joy?" We can smile and say with 100 percent certainty, "That's not me. That's Jesus in me." The gift we've been given is that He would choose us, live within us, and use us to shine His Light to a dark, dark world.

EXTRA VERSES FOR STUDY OR PRAYER

Genesis 1:3–4; Acts 9:15; Galatians 2:20

VERSE OF THE DAY

For God, who said, "Let light shine out of darkness," has shone in our hearts to give the light of the knowledge of the glory of God in

the face of Jesus Christ. But we have this treasure in jars of clay, to show that the surpassing power belongs to God and not to us.
—2 Corinthians 4:6–7

PRAYER

Father, we have nothing to recommend ourselves. We are like common clay pots You have chosen to fill with Your glorious Light. Please shine through us so that others will know that this is not from us but You. In Jesus's name, amen.

THINK

PRAY

PRAISE

TO-DO

PRAYER LIST

QUESTIONS FOR DEEPER REFLECTION

1. Can you think of a simple or homespun Christmas memory that brought you joy?

2. How have you seen God shine through your weakness?

DAY 25

BEFORE AND AFTER

For at one time you were darkness,
but now you are light in the Lord.
Walk as children of light (for the fruit of light is
found in all that is good and right and true).
—Ephesians 5:8–9

If you are working your way through this devotional in the month of December and have been able to keep up while baking dozens of cookies, attending Christmas programs, and shopping for your loved ones, then today is Christmas Day. So let me be the first to say Merry Christmas. I hope you have a cup of something warm beside you and a Christmas cookie to enjoy. Maybe it is early morning, and you have tiptoed out of your bedroom to sit beside the Christmas tree, waiting for your family to join you. Or maybe the day was well spent, and you are squeezing out a few more minutes of contemplation before you collapse into bed. I think we can take a cue from Mary, the mother of Jesus, who looked around at the simple group of shepherds on that first Christmas night and took it all in. Luke said of her, *"But Mary treasured up all these things, pondering them in her heart"* (Luke 2:19). Truthfully, the older I get, the more Christmas has that treasuring and pondering effect on me. I can't help but be grateful for what Christmas means in a very real practical way in my life.

SOMETHING TO THINK ABOUT

We all love a good makeover. Nothing makes us happier than a chaotic mess of a house becoming a wondrous haven. Just so you know, if Joanna Gaines shows up at my house, you better believe I'm taking before and after pictures. Paul leans heavily on this idea in our verse of the day when he says, *"At one time you were darkness, but now you are light."* Did you notice what he said? Not you were *in* darkness or darkness was all around you, but *"you **were** darkness."* This is a strong statement. It means that everything that was true of darkness was true of you. You sat in chaos. You were empty. You lacked wisdom and understanding. Darkness had a grip on you and permeated every part of your life. You were hopeless.

But now something has changed. *"Now you are light in the Lord."* You have been transformed from darkness to light. Your very identity is characterized by light because you have been filled with Jesus—the eternal Light of the world. He came in and turned on His light in your life. You have access to His Spirit, who will teach you how to walk in a way that honors Him. What does this look like in our daily lives? It means that you can clearly see evidence of goodness, righteousness, and truth radiating in and through our lives. The *after* pictures are stunning because we look like Jesus.

What does Christmas mean to me? It means that I *was* darkness, but now because of the incarnation of Jesus and His gift of salvation, I *am* light in the Lord. Before and after. What a gift to treasure and ponder.

EXTRA VERSES FOR STUDY OR PRAYER
Ephesians 2:1–3; 1 John 1:5–6

VERSE OF THE DAY

For at one time you were darkness, but now you are light in the Lord. Walk as children of light (for the fruit of light is found in all that is good and right and true). —Ephesians 5:8–9

PRAYER

Father, thank You for the incarnation of Your Son, Jesus, the Light of the world, who has come into my life and transformed me from darkness to light in Him. May my life reflect all that is good, right, and true. In Jesus's name, amen.

THINK

PRAY

PRAISE

TO-DO   PRAYER LIST

QUESTIONS FOR DEEPER REFLECTION

1. How can you treasure and ponder the gift of *before and after* in your life?

2. What is one memory from Christmas this year that you want to remember? Record it here in as much detail as possible with the date and year. Next Christmas, add another and so on.

THE LIGHT BRINGS UNEXPECTED GIFTS

Therefore do not pronounce judgment before the time, before the Lord comes, who will bring to light the things now hidden in darkness and will disclose the purposes of the heart. Then each one will receive his commendation from God.
—1 Corinthians 4:5

I've discovered over the years that I have the strength of responsibility. According to *StrengthsFinder 2.0* this means that I take psychological ownership for anything I commit to and I feel emotionally bound to follow it through to completion.[11] On a good day, this simply means I get things done. I am dependable and committed to anything that might have my name attached to it. On not so good days, I tend to volunteer for more than I can handle. Saying "no" as a complete sentence is a challenge for me. I have also been known to take responsibility for other people's work.

As a result, I have wondered at times if this strength is a gift or a curse. It frequently feels like a weight I carry around in the center of my heart. My daughter Emma likes to remind me that only Jesus embodies every one of the thirty-four strengths with perfection. And since I am certainly not perfect, I will not come close to the mark. But I don't have to, thank goodness. James 1:17 tells us, *"Every good gift and every perfect gift is from above, coming down from the Father of*

---

11. Tom Rath, *StrengthsFinder 2.0* (New York: Gallop Press, 2007), 149.

lights, with whom there is no variation or shadow due to change." And when I resist my tendency to take my responsibility strength to the extreme, I can find joy in this gift.

SOMETHING TO THINK ABOUT

Have you ever thought about the gifts that we have in Christ Jesus besides salvation? Paul writes to the Corinthian church about one such unexpected gift. He tells them that they do not need to pass judgment on anyone, good or bad. When the Lord comes, He will illuminate the secret things hidden in the darkness and reveal the motives of every heart. Some of those secret things are worthy of judgment, and He will take care of those. Other motives are beautiful but hidden, and they will be given a share of praise by God Himself. The gift for us is that it isn't up to us to decide between the two. We don't bear the responsibility of making sure every bad deed is punished and every good deed is praised. That belongs to the Lord. And the promise we have is that when He comes, He will draw out everything into the light.

I don't know about you, but this Christmas, I want to celebrate this gift. I want to look forward to the day when the praise that comes my way for any strength I have will be from God and not from men. When it comes from Him, that is the only praise that truly matters.

EXTRA VERSES FOR STUDY OR PRAYER

First Samuel 16:7; Jeremiah 11:20; James 1:17

VERSE OF THE DAY

Therefore do not pronounce judgment before the time, before the Lord comes, who will bring to light the things now hidden in darkness and will disclose the purposes of the heart. Then each one will receive his commendation from God.

—1 Corinthians 4:5

PRAYER

Father, I want to resist the urge to take responsibility for things that are not mine to hold on to. I want to lean into the good gift that when You come again, You will bring everything good and bad into the light. In the meantime, use my good gifts for Your glory now and forever. In Jesus's name, amen.

THINK

PRAY

PRAISE

TO-DO

PRAYER LIST

QUESTIONS FOR DEEPER REFLECTION

1. What strength do you have that reflects the image of God? How do you use it for His glory?

    ----

2. How does knowing that when Jesus returns, He will bring everything to light feel like a gift to you today?

DAY 27

ACT LIKE YOU BELONG TO SOMEBODY

That you may be blameless and innocent,
children of God without blemish in the midst of
a crooked and twisted generation,
among whom you shine as lights in the world.
—Philippians 2:15

I might be rocking the Christmas boat a bit by admitting this, but our family did not promote the story of Santa Claus for our kids when they were growing up. It wasn't like we sat them down one day and revealed any big secret; we just chose to focus on the coming of Jesus. I have wondered if I robbed my girls of childhood imagination or caused them distress when most of their playmates were going to the mall to sit on Santa's lap to tell him what they wanted for Christmas. I assure you, they had a very detailed Christmas list with URLs and pictures of everything they wanted to be under the tree on Christmas Day. And much of the time, they found what their hearts desired on Christmas morning thanks to Grandma.

Our decision to shift the focus of the season had more to do with my experience growing up and how utterly devastated I was in fourth grade when I found out the truth. I didn't want my girls to put their hopes on a person who didn't exist—or at least didn't exist in the way our culture promotes. In college, I wrote a paper on St. Nicholas; I learned that the legend is based on a real man of faith who loved God with his whole heart. It influenced the way he lived his life and made an impact on those he served.

SOMETHING TO THINK ABOUT

Because we didn't focus on the guy in the red suit, we didn't have the *leverage* at Christmastime of saying, "Remember, Santa is coming to town, so you better behave." I know this is not a great parenting strategy to begin with, but honestly, who hasn't offered a bribe to their kids at some point. Maybe your family celebrates Santa, and this is a familiar refrain. There is absolutely no judgment coming from me on that! However, in our home, one thing I have reminded my girls is to act like they belong to somebody. When I've taken them to school, camp, or a friend's house, I would say, "Remember, you have a last name. And you carry it with you wherever you go. You are deeply loved, and you belong to us. Now act like it." I wanted my girls to know that they were not just loved and part of our family, but they represented our family name everywhere they went. And we wanted the Thacker name to be thought of well.

The apostle Paul often slipped into the role of spiritual father with the churches he served and communicated with regularly. He made a habit of reminding them that they belonged to their heavenly Father, and he wanted them to act like it. This meant they were to make sure they didn't do anything that would deserve censure. He challenged them to be uncorrupted by the world around them. Their lives were to be *"a breath of fresh air in this squalid and polluted society"* (Philippians 2:15 MSG). How would they do this? Paul reminded them to:

- Do everything without grumbling or complaining
- Live clean lives
- Hold fast to the Word of God

Paul encouraged them to do these things and when Jesus returned, he would be proud of them. That's good spiritual parenting right there. God's kids don't complain. God's kids live clean lives.

God's kids hold to and share His lifegiving Word. When we remember these exhortations, we can act like we belong to somebody too. And He is the best of all Fathers.

EXTRA VERSES FOR STUDY OR PRAYER

Ephesians 1:4; 1 Thessalonians 5:18; Hebrews 10:23

VERSE OF THE DAY

That you may be blameless and innocent, children of God without blemish in the midst of a crooked and twisted generation, among whom you shine as lights in the world.

—Philippians 2:15

PRAYER

Father, thank You for making me Your daughter and giving me a new name. May my life always honor You. Help me to give thanks and not grumble, live a clean life free from sin, and hold unswervingly to the promises in Your Word. In Jesus's name, amen.

THINK

PRAY

PRAISE

_____

_____

_____

TO-DO

_____

_____

_____

PRAYER LIST

_____

_____

_____

QUESTIONS FOR DEEPER REFLECTION

1. What was on your Christmas list this year? Did you get everything you wanted? Were you surprised by something that was or wasn't under the tree this year?

_____

_____

_____

2. What do you struggle with the most: grumbling, living free from a besetting sin, or holding fast to the Word of God? Remember that you belong to God. You are His child, and you carry His name. Live out of His love!

_____

_____

_____

DAY 28

THE SECOND ADVENT

For you are all children of light,
children of the day.
We are not of the night or of the darkness.
—1 Thessalonians 5:5

We have spent a fair amount of time over the past few weeks talking about the first Advent. If you remember, I shared with you that *advent* comes from the Latin word *adventus*, which means "to come." At Christmas, we celebrate that Jesus came into the world, took on flesh, and walked among us. The writer of Hebrews tells us the reason why:

> *Since therefore the children share in flesh and blood, he himself likewise partook of the same things, that through death he might destroy the one who has the power of death, that is, the devil, and deliver all those who through fear of death were subject to lifelong slavery.* —Hebrews 2:14–15

The first Advent is a beautiful reminder that Jesus was willing to become like us, with flesh and blood, so that through His death, He could destroy the power of death and the devil. Glory hallelujah! No wonder we celebrate for the entire month of December. We should probably consider extending our celebration long past December 25. Or at least leave the Christmas tree up until after the first of January as a reminder. He is worthy of our worship.

SOMETHING TO THINK ABOUT

As good as the first Advent was, the second Advent is going to be even better. After Jesus died and rose from the grave, He ascended into heaven. His followers stood around, looking up at the sky in bewilderment. I can't say I blame them. As they stood there, an angel of the Lord appeared to them and told them Jesus would come again the same way they saw Him go to heaven. This is the second Advent. Jesus Himself told His followers about this. In Mark 13:26, He said when He returned, they would see Him *"coming in clouds with great power and glory."* For now, we live in between these two comings, and we wait.

And while we wait, we live as children of the light. To be a child of something or someone means we carry their characteristics with us. My girls all look like me. They carry my mannerisms (or so they've been told), and they sound like me. This is mostly a good thing. And though they may cringe when they hear it, I smile when someone says my daughters are like me. But what I love even more is when I get to pull them into a hug and speak an even more important truth over them. I remind them: "Remember, you are a daughter of the day. You are not a daughter of darkness. You are light. Darkness has no power over you."

Why do I do this? Because I want my girls to look forward to the future. I want them to be hopeful. And I want them to know that they are light bearers and darkness does not win.

I want this for you too. As a child of day, light is your defining characteristic. And no wonder. You are a child of the Light of the world. He is coming back. Soon. And when He does, light will once again flood the sky, and we will be ready.

EXTRA VERSES FOR STUDY OR PRAYER

Mark 12:26; Acts 1:11; Hebrews 2:14–15

VERSE OF THE DAY

For you are all children of light, children of the day. We are not of the night or of the darkness. —1 Thessalonians 5:5

PRAYER

Father, we are looking forward to Jesus's return with hope. While we wait, help us to remember our distinguishing characteristic is that we are children of light. And darkness has no power over us. In Jesus's name, amen.

THINK

PRAY

PRAISE

TO-DO

PRAYER LIST

QUESTIONS FOR DEEPER REFLECTION

1. How do others say you resemble your parents?

   _____

   _____

   _____

2. Light a candle tonight and spend some time quietly reflecting on how you are a daughter of the day and light is your defining characteristic. Write a prayer of gratitude to the Lord.

   _____

   _____

   _____

DAY 29

OUR SPECIAL JOB

But you are a chosen race, a royal priesthood,
a holy nation, a people for his own possession,
that you may proclaim the excellencies of him
who called you out of darkness into his marvelous light.
—1 Peter 2:9

There are quite a few social media memes about the week between Christmas and New Year's. Most of them speak to the idea that this is the week that you don't know who you are, what day it is, or what you are supposed to be doing. It makes me laugh because it is 100 percent true for me. This week feels like running into a brick wall of nothingness. The Norwegians have a name for this week. It's called *Romjul*.

> *Romjul* is a Norwegian holiday that refers to the week as a tranquil time to spend at home with friends and family undisturbed by the outside world. And a great time to rest, recharge and reset for the new year. The British equivalent is Boxing Week and I love the Danish term, "Yule Vacation."[12]

After the typical busyness of the Christmas season, it can be wonderful to cozy up with your family, read a book, and rest. Once I recover from hitting the brick wall at full speed, I find this week a

---

12. Amy Slenker-Smith, "How to Romjul – Guide to the Week Between Christmas and New Years," December 25, 2024, www.simplyenough.net/romjul.

great time to reflect on the past year and take some time to dream about what God wants for me in the coming season.

SOMETHING TO THINK ABOUT

As you are resting and recharging this week, remember that as a Christ follower, you are the dwelling place of God. Before Jesus came to earth, God's dwelling place was a building—first a tabernacle (tent) and then the temple. But now, through Christ's death and resurrection and the power of the Holy Spirit, God dwells in human hearts. It's a big deal to be called people who belong to God. But this calling also comes with a mission. We have something we are supposed to be doing. As God's people, our job is to declare His goodness to the world. (See Matthew 28:19–20.) We get to show and tell everyone what He has done for us. I love this translation of today's verse:

> *But you are the ones chosen by God, chosen for the high calling of priestly work, chosen to be a holy people, God's instruments to do his work and speak out for him, to tell others of the night-and-day difference he made for you.*　　　　—1 Peter 2:9 MSG

Has God made a night and day difference in your life? Talk about it.

Has He changed you? Put that on social media.

Were you once rejected and now you are accepted? Praise His Holy name.

That's our special job. It's our assignment. It's perfectly fine if you take a nap first. This week is tailor-made for it. But on January 2, when you head back to work, your kids go back to school, or you find yourself returning Christmas gifts that weren't quite right, be sure to share the goodness of God with someone. It just might change their life.

EXTRA VERSES FOR STUDY OR PRAYER

Psalm 73:28; John 1:14; Colossians 1:12

VERSE OF THE DAY

But you are a chosen race, a royal priesthood, a holy nation, a people for his own possession, that you may proclaim the excellencies of him who called you out of darkness into his marvelous light. —1 Peter 2:9

PRAYER

Father, thank You for making my heart Your home. I am ready to show others Your goodness and how You moved me out of darkness into Your amazing life-giving light. It's a story I love to tell. In Jesus's name, amen.

THINK

PRAY

PRAISE

TO-DO

PRAYER LIST

QUESTIONS FOR DEEPER REFLECTION

1. How are you spending the week between Christmas and New Year's?

    _____

    _____

    _____

2. What do you think God wants to do through your one beautiful life in the coming year?

    _____

    _____

    _____

DAY 30

WALKING
IN THE LIGHT

But if we walk in the light, as he is in the light,
we have fellowship with one another,
and the blood of Jesus his Son cleanses us from all sin.
—1 John 1:7

My daughter (who was five years old at the time) must have been chattering to me for several minutes. I was a bit distracted, but I could have sworn I heard her say "Borneo" and something about chickens. "Mommy!" she exclaimed louder than before. "I want to give my birthday present for Jesus to Borneo." What? Did my five-year-old just say Borneo? "Okay, honey, let's see what we can do," I said while googling where in the world Borneo was located. (It's a large island in Southeast Asia that's part of Malaysia and Indonesia.) "Okay, sweetie," I told her. "Mommy has a friend who is a missionary in Indonesia. I will send her an email and ask her how close she lives to Borneo. Maybe she can help us out."

Let me explain what initiated this conversation that happens every Christmas at our home. During our seasonal Advent celebration, we give our girls small gifts each week. But on Christmas Eve, instead of giving them a gift, they choose a gift to give to Jesus just like the wise men who brought gifts for the newborn king. And over the years, our family has given money to build wells in Africa, support homes for expectant mothers in other countries, helped a family who was going through a hard time, and supported local ministries that partner with our church. But this year, out of nowhere, my daughter wanted to give chickens to someone in Borneo, Indonesia.

As it turned out, my friend lived in Borneo. My five-year-old was not surprised. She knew God was in this. Through a discussion via email, I explained our tradition of giving our girls $30 on Christmas Eve to buy a gift for Jesus. I told her my five-year-old wanted to give her birthday gift for Jesus to Borneo. She replied with a couple of choices for my girl, and she chose, you guessed it, chickens. My friend told me that the local woman receiving the chickens recently had her chickens stolen. Not only would this help her, but it would also grow her business bigger than before.

SOMETHING TO THINK ABOUT

Did you know that walking in the light has a beautiful byproduct? First John 1:7 says when we walk in the light, we have fellowship with others who are also walking in the light. The word for *fellowship* here is the Greek word *koinónia*, which means "fellowship, communion, participation, sharing."[13] Basically, it means we share our lives. What makes this possible is that we first share our lives with Jesus, who is the perfect embodiment of light. And as we walk with Him, we are transformed. We become like Him. We look like Him. We act like Him. We think like Him. We give generously like Him. It doesn't mean we are perfect. It means that as we walk with Jesus and participate in community with other believers, we can trust the blood of Jesus to wash us clean and keep us well connected to others.

I've heard people say, "I love Jesus, but His people are another story." I get it. Church people can be difficult. We are all sinners saved by grace and sometimes, we put that grace to the test. And even though I understand the bad rap the church sometimes gets, maybe we could recognize when we get it right, which happens more than we realize, I think. It happens when we notice a single mom at church who needs money for her groceries. It happens when we stop and

---

13. G2842. koinónia. *Strong's Greek Concordance.*

pray with someone we know is hurting. It also happens when we celebrate a new believer's baptism or serve in a preschool classroom. And yes, it happens when a five-year-old gives Jesus a birthday present that results in a woman in Borneo restarting her chicken business. Walking in the light brings us into a life-giving, beautiful community with others who are walking in the light too. And it is a blessing. Let's encourage each other with these truths.

EXTRA VERSES FOR STUDY OR PRAYER

Matthew 2:10–11; Acts 2:42; 1 John 1:3

VERSE OF THE DAY

But if we walk in the light, as he is in the light, we have fellowship with one another, and the blood of Jesus his Son cleanses us from all sin. —1 John 1:7

PRAYER

Father, thank You that I can walk with You in the light. Please help me make progress and look more like You every day. Thank You for other believers who walk in the light with me. Let me share my life with them in a way that blesses them and honors You. In Jesus's name, amen.

THINK

PRAY

PRAISE

_____

_____

_____

TO-DO

_____

_____

_____

PRAYER LIST

_____

_____

_____

QUESTIONS FOR DEEPER REFLECTION

1. What does it mean to you to walk in the light with Jesus? With others?

_____

_____

_____

2. How have you shared your life this Christmas season?

_____

_____

_____

DAY 31

THE
EVERLASTING LIGHT

And the city has no need of sun or moon to shine on it, for the glory of God gives it light, and its lamp is the Lamb.
—Revelation 21:23

Years ago, I heard about an unbelievable light display you could only see once a year at the most magical place on earth. *The Osborne Family Spectacle of Dancing Lights* became a beloved Disney World main attraction from 1995–2016.[14] Housed on the Hollywood Studios backlot, it featured five million lights, festive holiday music, and several hidden Mickeys for onlookers to discover. Originally owned by the Osborne family of Little Rock, Arkansas, it started when their daughter Allison asked her dad to decorate their family home for Christmas. He took the challenge to another level and ended up donating it to Disney when it grew big enough to be seen from outer space, drew thousands of visitors, solicited complaints from angry neighbors, and eventually involved the Supreme Court.

My family was able to visit Disney at Christmas one year—being a local does have its advantages!—and experience the lights. I say experience because the best part was being present when the display was switched on each night. You can't help but "ooh" and "awe" when five million lights illuminate the dark December night all at once.

---

14. Brian Delpozo, "The Complete History of the Osborne Family Spectacle of Dancing Lights," November 22, 2020, allears.net/2020/11/22/the-complete-history-of-the-osborne-family-spectacle-of-dancing-lights.

It was truly a sight to see. My Florida girls also loved the fake snow that Disney (of course) added to the mix. It was a sweet memory for my family and one I can still see in my mind's eye when I picture that joyous night together.

SOMETHING TO THINK ABOUT

Chasing the theme of Light through the Scriptures has brought us to the last book of the Bible and a glimpse of an unbelievable yet true vision of what we will experience in the new heaven and the new earth. God's city will come down from heaven and be a stunning sight to see—like *"a bride adorned for her husband"* (Revelation 21:2). God Himself will dwell in the city with His people. There will be no more tears. No more death. And no more pain. This city will have the glory of God within it, *"its radiance like a most rare jewel"* (verse 11). But here, in these final pages of the Word, we also learn that the city of God will not need the sun or the moon (or five million man-made lights for that matter) to light up the sky. It will be lit with the glory of God, and the lamp of the city will be the Lamb.

This should come as no surprise to us. John—the author of Revelation, three letters (1, 2, and 3 John), and the Gospel of John has already told us that Jesus is the Lamb of God who takes away the sins of the world. He is the Light of the world, and He came as the eternal light. But lest we think John is the only one who was given this insight, we also have seen this language in the prophetic words of Isaiah chapter 60. We had a hint on day 9:

> *Arise, shine, for your light has come, and the glory of the* Lord *has risen upon you.*   —Isaiah 60:1

And later, in the same chapter, the prophet says:

> *The sun shall be no more your light by day, nor for brightness shall the moon give you light; but the* Lord *will be your everlasting light, and your God will be your glory.*   —Isaiah 60:19

Of course, you probably remember in Genesis 1 that God gave us the sun and moon to rule over our days and nights. But now we see that God's glory is even better. It is continuous. His glory removes every trace of darkness. Why are there no more tears? No pain? And no more death? Because God's glory eradicates sin as well.

Friends, the eternal city of God will be all about His glory. The Lamb—who came as a baby at Christmas, was wrapped in swaddling clothes, laid in a manger, lived a perfect, light-filled life, died for our sins, and rose from the grave—will sit on the eternal throne forever and ever.

> *By its light will the nations walk, and the kings of the earth will bring their glory into it, and its gates will never be shut by day— and there will be no night there.*   —Revelation 21:24–25

The gates will never be shut by day, and there will be no night.

Joy to the world. The Lord is come.

EXTRA VERSES FOR STUDY OR PRAYER

Genesis 1:14–18; Isaiah 60:19; Revelation 22:1–5

VERSE OF THE DAY

And the city has no need of sun or moon to shine on it, for the glory of God gives it light, and its lamp is the Lamb.
                                        —Revelation 21:23

PRAYER

Father, from the beginning, You gave us light to draw a boundary to the darkness. You used it to show us the way to go, to give us understanding, and to reveal deep and hidden truths in Your Word. Jesus, the Light of the world, illuminated the darkness in our hearts and took away our sin. His light is what transforms us, lets others know we are Your children, and how we reflect Your glory to others. May we remember today that Your Light is the gift that is to be experienced, enjoyed, and shared every day of the year. In Jesus's name, amen.

THINK

PRAY

PRAISE

TO-DO   PRAYER LIST

---   ---
---   ---
---   ---

QUESTIONS FOR DEEPER REFLECTION

1. When you started this devotional, did you have any idea how consistent the theme of light is throughout all of Scripture? What does this communicate to you about the character of God?

---

2. What is one takeaway about light that you want to reflect on as you go into the new year?

APPENDIX

CHRISTMAS SONGS TO SING[15]

O HOLY NIGHT

By Adolphe Adam, 1847

O holy night! the stars are brightly shining;
It is the night of the dear Savior's birth.
Long lay the world in sin and error pining,
Till He appeared and the soul felt its worth.
A thrill of hope—the weary world rejoices,
For yonder breaks a new and glorious morn!
Fall on your knees! O hear the angel voices!
O night divine, O night when Christ was born!
O night, O holy night, O night divine!

Led by the light of faith serenely beaming,
With glowing hearts by His cradle we stand.
So led by light of a star sweetly gleaming,
Here came the Wise Men from Orient land.
The King of kings lay thus in lowly manger,
In all our trials born to be our Friend.
He knows our need—to our weakness is no stranger.

---

15. All of these songs are in the public domain.

Behold your King, before Him lowly bend!
Behold your King, before Him lowly bend!

Truly He taught us to love one another;
His law is love and His gospel is peace.
Chains shall He break, for the slave is our brother,
And in His name all oppression shall cease.
Sweet hymns of joy in grateful chorus raise we;
Let all within us praise His holy name.
Christ is the Lord! O praise His name forever!
His pow'r and glory evermore proclaim!
His pow'r and glory evermore proclaim!

COME THOU LONG EXPECTED JESUS [MENTIONED ON DAY 12]

By Charles Wesley, 1744

Come, Thou long expected Jesus,
Born to set Thy people free;
From our fears and sins release us,
Let us find our rest in Thee.
Israel's strength and consolation,
Hope of all the earth Thou art;
Dear desire of every nation,
Joy of every longing heart.

Born Thy people to deliver,
Born a child and yet a King,
Born to reign in us forever,
Now Thy gracious kingdom bring.
By Thine own eternal spirit
Rule in all our hearts alone;
By Thine all sufficient merit,
Raise us to Thy glorious throne.

HARK THE HERALD ANGELS SING

By Charles Wesley, 1739

Hark! the herald angels sing,
"Glory to the newborn King:
Peace on earth, and mercy mild,
God and sinners reconciled!"
Joyful, all ye nations, rise,
Join the triumph of the skies;
With th'angelic hosts proclaim,
"Christ is born in Bethlehem!"
Refrain:
Hark! the herald angels sing,
"Glory to the newborn King"

Christ, by highest heaven adored,
Christ, the everlasting Lord,
Late in time behold Him come,
Offspring of the Virgin's womb:
Veiled in flesh the Godhead see;
Hail th'incarnate Deity,
Pleased with us in flesh to dwell,
Jesus, our Immanuel. *[Refrain]*

Hail the heaven-born Prince of Peace!
Hail the Sun of Righteousness!
Light and life to all He brings,
Risen with healing in His wings.
Mild He lays His glory by,
Born that we no more may die,
Born to raise us from the earth,
Born to give us second birth. *[Refrain]*

SILENT NIGHT [MENTIONED DAY 17]

By Joseph Mohr, 1818

Silent night! Holy night!
All is calm, all is bright
'Round yon virgin mother and child!
Holy infant, so tender and mild,
Sleep in heavenly peace,
Sleep in heavenly peace.

Silent night! Holy night!
Shepherds quake at the sight.
Glories stream from heaven afar,
Heav'nly hosts sing, "Alleluia!
Christ the Savior is born!
Christ the Savior is born!"

Silent night! Holy night!
Son of God, love's pure light
Radiant beams from Thy holy face
With the dawn of redeeming grace,
Jesus, Lord, at Thy birth!
Jesus, Lord, at Thy birth!

Silent night! Holy night!
Wondrous star, lend thy light;
With the angels let us sing
"Alleluia" to our King:
"Christ the Savior is born!
Christ the Savior is born."

O COME O COME EMMANUEL

By J. M. Neale, 1851

O come, O come, Immanuel,
And ransom captive Israel
That mourns in lonely exile here
Until the Son of God appear.

Refrain:
Rejoice! Rejoice! Immanuel
Shall come to you, O Israel.

O come, O Wisdom from on high,
Who ordered all things mightily;
To us the path of knowledge show
And teach us in its ways to go. *[Refrain]*

JOY TO THE WORLD

By Issa Watts, 1719

Joy to the world, the Lord is come!
Let earth receive her King!
Let every heart prepare Him room,
And heav'n and nature sing,
And heav'n and nature sing,
And heav'n, and heav'n and nature sing.

Joy to the earth, the Savior reigns!
Let men their songs employ,
While fields and floods, rocks, hills, and plains
Repeat the sounding joy,
Repeat the sounding joy,
Repeat, repeat the sounding joy.

No more let sins and sorrows grow,
Nor thorns infest the ground;
He comes to make His blessings flow
Far as the curse is found,
Far as the curse is found,
Far as, far as the curse is found.

He rules the world with truth and grace,
And makes the nations prove
The glories of His righteousness
And wonders of His love,
And wonders of His love,
And wonders, wonders of His love.

ABOUT THE AUTHOR

Stacey Thacker has long served women and girls in ministry. A respected prayer mentor and Bible teacher and the author of ten books, she is a popular conference speaker, ministry director, and founder of Stacey Thacker Creative, where she works with top-selling authors and creatives.

Her books include *Praying for Teen Girls: Partner with God for the Heart of Your Daughter* and *Threadbare Prayer: Prayers for Hearts That Feel Hidden, Hurt, or Hopeless.*

Stacey also serves as the director of women's ministry at First Orlando. She received her B.A. in Sociology from Indiana University.

She lives in central Florida with her husband Mike and four daughters. To connect with Stacey, visit StaceyThacker.com.